THE
INTIMATE
INTERIORS
OF
Edouard Vuillard

THE INTIMATE INTERIORS OF

ELIZABETH WYNNE EASTON

THE MUSEUM OF FINE ARTS   HOUSTON

Edouard Vuillard

BY THE SMITHSONIAN INSTITUTION PRESS   WASHINGTON

Published on the occasion of the exhibition
The Intimate Interiors of Edouard Vuillard

The Museum of Fine Arts, Houston
18 November 1989 – 29 January 1990

The Phillips Collection
Washington, D.C.
17 February 1990 – 29 April 1990

The Brooklyn Museum
18 May 1990 – 30 July 1990

© 1989 Smithsonian Institution
© 1989 The Museum of Fine Arts, Houston:
text and illustrations
Library of Congress Cataloging-in-Publication
Data
Easton, Elizabeth Wynne.
The intimate interiors of Edouard Vuillard/
Elizabeth Wynne Easton.
p.   cm.
The Museum of Fine Arts, Houston,
18 November 1989 – 29 January 1990;
the Phillips Collection, Washington, D.C.,
17 February 1990 – 29 April 1990;
The Brooklyn Museum,
18 May 1990 – 30 July 1990.
Bibliography: p.
Includes index.
ISBN 0-87474-402-4 (alk. paper).—
ISBN 0-87474-427-X (pbk. alk. paper)
1. Vuillard, Edouard, 1868–1940—Exhibitions.
2. Interiors in art—Exhibitions.
I. Museum of Fine Arts, Houston.
II. Phillips Collection. III. Brooklyn Museum.
IV. Title.
ND553.V9A4   1989   759.4—dc20
89-600069   CIP
British Library Cataloging-in-Publication Data
available
∞ The paper used in this publication meets the
minimum requirements of the American National Standard for Permanence of Paper for
Printed Library Materials Z39.48-1984.
Manufactured in Japan
10 9 8 7 6 5 4 3 2 1

Cover: Edouard Vuillard, *Interior with Women
Sewing (L'Aiguillée),* 1893, oil on canvas, 15⅞ x
12¹¹⁄₁₆ in., Yale University Art Gallery, New
Haven, Connecticut; gift of Mr. and Mrs. Paul
Mellon, B.A. 1929; and *Child in a Room,* c.
1900, oil on cardboard, 17¼ x 22¾ in.,
© 1989 The Art Institute of Chicago; Mr. and
Mrs. Martin A. Ryerson Collection.

Frontispiece: Edouard Vuillard, *The Atelier,*
1892, oil on canvas, 18¼ x 45½ in., private
collection, New York.

The exhibition was organized by

The Museum of Fine Arts, Houston

and made possible by

generous grants from

Mr. and Mrs. Meredith J. Long

and from the

National Endowment for the Arts.

To Anne Coffin Hanson and James Stuart Traub

CONTENTS

LENDERS TO THE EXHIBITION

The Art Institute of Chicago

Herbert Black, Canada

Private Collection of Jane Forbes Clark

Dumbarton Oaks Research Library and Collection, Washington, D.C.

Aaron Fleischman, Washington, D.C.

Galerie Jan Krugier: Geneva

Mrs. Samuel Godfrey

Hirshhorn Museum and Sculpture Garden, Smithsonian Institution, Washington, D.C.

Indianapolis Museum of Art

Josefowitz Collection

Kunstmuseum Winterthur, Switzerland

The Metropolitan Museum of Art, New York

Musée de l'Annonciade, Saint-Tropez

Museu de Arte de São Paolo, Brazil

The Museum of Modern Art, New York

National Gallery of Art, Washington, D.C.

The Philadelphia Museum of Art

The Phillips Collection, Washington, D.C.

Rose Art Museum, Brandeis University, Waltham, Massachusetts

The Saint Louis Art Museum

San Francisco Museum of Modern Art

Collection S.

Scottish National Gallery of Modern Art, Edinburgh

William Kelly Simpson

Smith College Museum of Art, Northampton, Massachusetts

Beverly Sommer, New York

Staatsgalerie Stuttgart

Wallraf-Richartz-Museum, Cologne

Malcolm Wiener, New York

Mrs. John Hay Whitney, New York

Yale University Art Gallery, New Haven, Connecticut

Gustav Zumsteg, Zurich

Private collections

FOREWORD

*O*ne hundred years ago Edouard Vuillard, then only twenty years old, was about to embark on a career as a painter. Following the route of many an aspiring artist, he had been to the Ecole des Beaux-Arts and he was still going every day to the Louvre to study the paintings of the old masters. No one could have predicted that in three years Vuillard would be painting works that challenged the very principles by which paintings had been made since the Renaissance.

This exhibition offers some of Vuillard's greatest paintings from the 1890s, that first and crucial phase of his career. We hope that it will provide a rare opportunity for connoisseurs, historians, and all who love great painting to understand the extent of Vuillard's achievement in those years.

Elizabeth Easton, assistant curator of European paintings at The Brooklyn Museum, has chosen the works in the exhibition and has written the book that accompanies it. She has worked closely with George T. M. Shackelford, our curator of European painting and sculpture, throughout the project. We are grateful to them and to the staff of the Museum of Fine Arts, Houston, for bringing this rich and thoughtful exhibition to completion. Generous grants from Mr. and Mrs. Meredith J. Long and from the National Endowment for the Arts made the exhibition and book possible.

With our colleagues at The Phillips Collection, Washington, D.C., and at The Brooklyn Museum, where the exhibition will be presented after it leaves Houston, we are most grateful to the museums and private collectors, in this country and abroad, who have agreed to lend their works to this show. They have enabled us to bring together a body of work that, we hope, will make a new generation see Vuillard's intimate interiors in a new light.

Peter C. Marzio
Director
The Museum of Fine Arts, Houston

ACKNOWLEDGMENTS

When I began my research on Edouard Vuillard eight years ago, I hardly dreamed that it would someday result in an exhibition. My deepest thanks therefore must go to George T. M. Shackelford, who suggested the possibility of this exhibition to me and whose devotion to the project ensured its success. I am also grateful to Peter C. Marzio, The Museum of Fine Arts, Houston; Laughlin Phillips, The Phillips Collection; Robert T. Buck, The Brooklyn Museum; and the trustees of all three institutions for this opportunity.

It is Anne Coffin Hanson whom I must thank for initially encouraging me to probe the intricacies of Edouard Vuillard's pictorial space in her noted graduate seminar at Yale University, which has inspired so many historians of art. Her critical but always supportive eye saw me through many revisions of my dissertation on Vuillard and equally many refinements in my thinking. Other teachers and fellow students from Yale helped my thoughts evolve, including Peter Nisbet and Richard Field, and especially Robert L. Herbert, whose insightful comments made my work more cohesive.

I was fortunate to receive several fellowships that enabled me to live in France to pursue my research. I am grateful to the Kress Foundation, the Fulbright Foundation, the Georges Lurcy Foundation, and The Metropolitan Museum of Art, where I was a Chester Dale fellow and an Andrew Mellon fellow. It was at that institution that I had the good fortune to meet Lucy Belloli, conservator of paintings. I have benefited

xiii

from her penetrating powers of observation and her technical expertise. It is my sincere hope that together we will be able to contribute to the knowledge of Vuillard's technique after examining the works in this exhibition.

Of course no study on Vuillard can ever be complete without the cooperation of Antoine Salomon. His knowledge of Vuillard's entire oeuvre is unparalleled, and his sensitivity to the paintings makes all scholars aware of Vuillard the man as well as of his work. I am truly recognizant of the time he has taken with me over the years, and I look forward to the publication of the long-awaited catalogue raisonné of Vuillard's work.

For all scholars of the 1890s, one of the greatest treats is getting to know the Josefowitz family. Sam Josefowitz is legendary for his kindness, generosity, and knowledge, and I count myself extremely lucky to have benefited from all three. Paul and Ellen Josefowitz also deserve thanks for their gracious hospitality and their help in locating pictures.

Among collectors few are so willing to share ideas and pictures as Kelly Simpson; I will always treasure his generosity. Special thanks are also due to Mrs. Donald Stralem, who let me visit her collection as often as I wished.

I am also grateful to François Daulte, for helping me to locate pictures in private collections, and to Juliet Wilson Bareau. Mme. Hautecoeur and Mme. Dumas, librarians of the Bibliothèque de l'Institut de France, graciously allowed me daily access to the Vuillard journals from 1981 to 1984.

Friends and colleagues who have given me advice and inspiration over the years are too numerous to mention, but several deserve a word of thanks: Colin Bailey, Hilary M. Ballon, Andrea Bayer, Emily Braun, Teresa Carbone, Katherine Cary, Gunnar Dahl, Ann Dumas, Yasmin Ergas, Leonard Groopman, Colta Ives, Jessica Katzenellenbogen, Elaine Koss, Caroline Milbank, Dr. Ursula Perucchi-Petri, Elizabeth Prelinger, Ruth Popper, Michael Rips, Anne H. Schirrmeister, Margaret Denton Smith, Christine van den Broek, and Eleanor Winthrop. Several art dealers and auction experts were of critical help in obtaining pictures, particularly William Acquavella, Jean Claude and Yann Bellier, Huguette Berès, Marianne Feilchenfeldt, Michael Fitzgerald and Michael Findlay, Thomas Gibson, Sabine Helms, Ay-Wang Hsia, Christian Naeff, Peter Nathan, Heidi Römer, Martin Summers, Patricia Tang and E. V. Thaw, and Diane Upright and Jan Krugier. I would like to give special thanks to Pat Coman and his staff at the Watson Library of The Metropolitan Museum of Art for their hospitality over the years.

Many departments at the Museum of Fine Arts, Houston, have contributed to the success of the exhibition and this book. I would like to thank the staffs of the curatorial, registrar's, publications, design and production, graphics, development, and public relations departments. I am particularly grateful to Mary Christian, who coordinated the photography for this book. I would also like to thank Wanda Allison, Karen Bremer, Charles Carroll, Sara Garcia, Celeste Marie Adams, Carolyn Vaughan, Polly Koch, Kathryn Kelley, Susan Giannantonio, Jack Eby, Lorri Lewis, Margaret

Skidmore, Barbara Michels, Ed Harris, and Anne Lewis.

At The Brooklyn Museum I would like to thank Sarah Faunce, chair of the department of painting and sculpture, Roy Eddey, deputy director, and Linda Ferber, chief curator, for their encouragement of this project. This exhibition would never have been possible without the enthusiastic support of Ken Moser, Kevin Stayton, and Barry Harwood. Karin Knight was responsible for the book's index and the rest of the conservation staff were helpful in countless ways. I am also grateful to Cathryn Anders, the art handlers, Larry Clark, Jennifer Hersh, Nancy Hood, Elizabeth Reynolds, Deborah Schwartz, Jeffrey Strean, Missy Sullivan, Richard Waller, and Rena Zurofsky.

My sincere thanks go to Sir Lawrence Gowing, Eliza Rathbone, Elizabeth Griffith, and Linda Johnson at The Phillips Collection. I am also grateful to the staff of the Smithsonian Institution Press, especially Amy Pastan, Leigh Alvarado Benson, Kathleen Brown, and Lisa Buck Vann.

Finally, I want to recognize the persevering support of my family, especially my mother, who lived through many years when Vuillard often took precedence. To them go my thanks and love.

To my husband, James Traub, goes all my heart, for he read every word of the manuscript and shared with me his wisdom. This would be less of a book, and a much longer one, without him.

E.W.E.

INTRODUCTION

*I*n 1891, Edouard Vuillard was at the beginning of his career as a painter and, paradoxically, at the height of his mastery of the craft. In a journal entry of April 2, he addressed ideas that were to remain central to his art throughout the remaining fifty years of his life: the relationship between form and color and their power to convey meaning independent of what they depict; the translation of sensation into a two-dimensional image; the depiction of powerful emotions in a work of art that conveys both the underlying complexity of the artist's intentions and his sense of artistic purpose; and how perception influences what the artist creates and what the viewer sees.

> . . . the way in which forms stand out from one another has this idea the relationship of light and as a consequence of color, also of form (occupied space) in which a form exists with that which surrounds it; "distinguish itself" would be better than "stand out," which implies the idea of distancing[;] this idea of distancing is an idea, not a primary sensation that is retained[.] I think I've seen an explanation mentioned: the eyes being two and at a certain distance one from the other. And so this feeling, the knowledge of this relationship is the Truth that it's necessary to have and which one will write on canvas or on paper. Without which if one hasn't got a model, a subject, one does the work of an insect strolling on paper with ink on its feet. What good is all this writing? If in raising my eyes to a painting or to nature I *will* to observe, I fall into falsity. One observes, one cannot will [oneself] to observe. The emotion contained therein (observation) alone can give—is the primary condition of—a work of art, before the spirit of

method and the practical intelligence that are born of the selfsame spirit that undergoes this emotion.[1]

These themes glimmer beneath the surface of Vuillard's work of the 1890s and are reflected in his writings throughout the decade. In his intimate interiors of this period, Vuillard's artistic sensibility is at its most sophisticated. These paintings, which evoke his life in a visual shorthand, both depict familiar rooms and convey his feelings toward the characters who peopled them. His pictorial construction, likewise, is at its most complex; the meaning of these works, nearly a century after their creation, remains elusive.

It is curious, in fact, how little we know today about Vuillard and his art. The outline of the painter's life is familiar: Vuillard was born in the provincial town of Cuiseaux in 1868, the youngest of three children who included his brother Alexandre and his sister Marie. His family moved to Paris in 1877, where he spent the remainder of his life.

Vuillard is famous, of course, as one of the founding members of the Nabi group, an influential offshoot of the Symbolist movement, which took its name from a Hebrew word for "prophet." His fellow Nabis included Ker-Xavier Roussel and Maurice Denis, whom he had known since his schoolboy days, and Félix Vallotton and Pierre Bonnard, whom he had met at the Académie Julian. They all began their stylistic innovations at about the same time as the famous Symbolist and Synthetist exhibition of the works of Paul Gauguin and his followers, which was held at the Café Volpini in 1889, and continued them throughout the nineties. Vuillard's most daring works in the Nabi style, however, date from the early years of the decade, less indebted to than rivaling Gauguin's innovations.

After the retrospective exhibition of Vuillard's art in 1971, with its comprehensive catalogue by John Russell, scholarship on the painter virtually ground to a halt in anticipation of the release to the public of his private journals. Now that these intimate documents have been made available for study, much more is known about this most private of the Nabi painters. Even with the information that the journals provide, however, Vuillard remains a secretive personality: the enigma of his mysterious interiors has not been resolved. For the admirer of his works, in fact, it is this elusiveness, this resistance, that makes them so compelling.

The exhibition and this book are intended to serve as a new and modest beginning to future investigations of Vuillard's art. Much remains to be done. The wealth of material in the journals will take years to absorb. The forthcoming catalogue raisonné, when published, also will add immeasurably to our understanding of the breadth of Vuillard's artistic experimentation.

For the present, however, the exhibition focuses on Vuillard's interiors of the 1890s, the works for which he is most famous. Of course, Vuillard painted for many decades after 1900 with great profusion and variety. His portraits, landscapes, and decorations of the 1890s also merit scholarly attention and popular admiration. The

2

decorations are particularly beautiful examples of the Nabi desire to escape the confines of the easel and, in this case, to embrace the architecture of the wall, glorying in the patterning and flatness that characterized decorative painting of the period. Nevertheless it is in Vuillard's small interiors that his artistic genius reaches its fullest flower. Although the decorations and the work after 1900 are beautiful, they do not achieve the same complexity of pictorial form nor the depth of psychological penetration that are at the core of Vuillard's easel paintings of the 1890s.

Vuillard has always been considered an intimist, not only because he preferred to paint small-scale pictures but also because he concentrated on evocative depictions of family and friends in familiar surroundings. Almost without exception, he chose interiors as the setting for the intimate subjects so close to his heart. Many of his larger decorative panels, on the other hand, depict panoramic landscapes or outdoor genre scenes. Made on commission, these works constitute a less private endeavor than the small easel pictures and lack the close weave and rich layering of the interiors.

In fact, Vuillard's choice of subject matter, and his attitude toward that subject, determined his format, composition, and spatial construction. Scenes of friends or family members, for example, usually are depicted on a small scale in an interior whose space is crowded and difficult to decipher. In contrast, the decorative panels seem to have encouraged Vuillard to open and flatten his space and to set his subjects out of doors.

Both the decorations and the small-scale easel pictures exhibited here frequently were rendered in Vuillard's beloved *peinture à la colle* (literally, "painting with glue"). Vuillard learned this process of combining pigment with heated glue by 1893, when he painted set decorations for the Théâtre de l'Oeuvre. Although most of his fellow Nabis also experimented with *peinture à la colle* for theatrical decors, Vuillard was the only one to expand his use of the medium to the rest of his painted oeuvre. In addition to a dry oil paint, which soaked into the cardboard or canvas, he used *peinture à la colle* to create an unprecedented flatness. There is still much to learn about how Vuillard chose his medium and whether his choice was determined by a given composition's subject matter or its size. Because so many of Vuillard's canvases have been varnished, these distinctions are difficult if not impossible to determine.

Vuillard's paintings and his life at times seem antithetical. His paintings offer claustrophobic glimpses into the intimate life of a bourgeois family in the last decade of the nineteenth century. Vuillard lived in Paris all his life, only occasionally traveling beyond its closest environs. His was a closely circumscribed world, especially during his formative years, and he grew up to be obsessed by the microcosm of the world around him. On the other hand, as a member of the intellectual and aesthetic avant-garde of the day, a friend to poets, playwrights, and publishers, Vuillard was part of a sophisticated circle that extended far beyond the walls of his family's apartment.

The interior, however, was the subject through which the young Vuillard could best explore the complex issues, both intellectual and emotional, which he grappled with in his first decade as a painter. The interior was for Vuillard a potential metaphor for himself—an inner space, self-controlled and cut off from the world, but rife with possibilities. In Vuillard's claustrophobic interiors of the 1890s, objects as well as gestures seem endowed with an inner life, and we feel the relentless psychological scrutiny of the painter. We have only to turn to the journal Vuillard kept during the same period for confirmation of his passionate exploration of the self.

The interior was also the locus of the home industry, a place where Vuillard observed the quiet dignity of labor and its characteristic gestures. But it was family life, confined within these ever-present walls, that aroused Vuillard's most powerful emotions. His interiors function as theaters within which the family enacted the consuming drama of everyday experience.

This book concentrates on Vuillard's pictorial construction: why he chose to depict his subjects in the way that he did. It also seeks to illuminate the social, economic, intellectual, and physical environment from which Vuillard's paintings evolved, approaching the work of art not only as an individual product of genius but as a document to be explained through historical research.

By looking at four specific areas of Vuillard's production—self-portraits, scenes of women sewing, images of family life, and paintings of his friend Misia Natanson—we hope to come to some understanding of the painter's subject matter and the way in which the pictures enagage in a complex dialogue. The vocabulary of the paintings has often been considered a private, indeed impenetrable, one. But by examining related paintings, both in juxtaposition and alone, we can eavesdrop on Vuillard's private conversation and recognize in the variety of images and settings a common language and a common theme.

4

denotes a work in the exhibition.

BEYOND THE MIRROR:

THE SELF-PORTRAITS

. . . conceive a picture as a series of accords . . .

EV I.2, 71v (31 August 1890)

1 🪰

Portrait of Vuillard and

Waroquy

1889–90

oil on canvas, 36½ x 28½ inches,

The Metropolitan Museum of Art, New

York; gift of Alex M. Lewyt, 1955

7

*E*very portrait comments in some way on the character of the sitter, but the self-portrait not only discloses the features and posture of the subject—the artist—but also links his image to his craft. A more intimate genre is scarcely imaginable than one in which subject and creator are one.

The fluctuating popularity of the self-portrait in the history of art provides a rough index to recurring periods of introspection and subjectivity. Literary and artistic self-reflection came to the forefront at the end of the nineteenth century, when the Symbolist aesthetic reigned. Both in technique and in spirit the late 1880s—when Edouard Vuillard began to develop as a painter—signaled a change in world view: artists began to reject the objective depiction of nature for which the Impressionists had fought. Artists and writers were replacing the related positivism of the philosopher Auguste Comte and the novelist Emile Zola with an emphasis on expressive equivalences and a desire to objectify in words or in paint the subjective states of intuition and imagination—in short, developing what we now call the Symbolist aesthetic.

Where the Impressionists recorded sensation, grounded in scientific fact and tempered by a Naturalist aesthetic, the Symbolist painters were concerned with perception, in which sensations were recorded through mental processes that varied according to each individual. Paul Gauguin and Georges Seurat were the first to explore this attitude toward picture making. Seurat contributed to a younger generation of artists that included Vuillard the idea that color and line convey meaning apart from the actual objects they describe. According to Seurat's often-cited program, upward-slanting lines and warm colors imbue a picture with happy sentiments, whereas down-turned lines and cool colors indicate sadness. Gauguin, for his part, encouraged artists to depart from academic depictions of nature and to choose colors in a free, subjective manner. Vuillard was particularly receptive to these suggestions following his education at the Lycée Condorcet in Paris.

Immanuel Kant's declaration in 1781 in the *Critique of Pure Reason* that there was no objective reality initiated the shift to the primacy of subjective experience. Almost a century later Kant's credo had worked its way into the basic corpus of ideas that was taught in the French *lycée* system, where it influenced the poets and philosophers who were Vuillard's peers. The notion of the supremacy of the individual, faith in perception as evidence of reality, belief in the relativity of truth, emphasis on the importance of observation and imagination, and use of analogy to strengthen a perceived truth were the staples of Vuillard's *lycée* education from the 1880s. These concepts also formed the core of the Symbolist doctrine. Thus, Vuillard's years in school not only introduced him to most of the artists who became the Nabi group but also provided the philosophical groundwork for his Symbolist aesthetic.[1]

Vuillard's earliest extant works, from about 1888, coincide with his first entries in a journal. His development as a painter therefore can be examined both through his painted works and his written record. Although he painted many still lifes and genre scenes in the late 1880s and early 1890s, none of these reveals his personality as do his portraits of himself. In these, as in his journals, Vuillard reflects on himself and his work.

Until recently, little was known of Vuillard's private thoughts. His historical place in late nineteenth-century French art, and his inclusion in the Nabi group in particular, has been based on written accounts by his contemporaries, primarily those by Maurice Denis, long recognized as the spokesman for the Nabis. Vuillard's journals, closed for forty years after his death, have now revealed to scholars the wide-ranging curiosity he brought to contemporary theory and the sophisticated level of his artistic inquiry.[2] His observations record the gradual development of an individual aesthetic in which color and line convey meaning apart from what they depict. Profusely illustrated from 1888 to about 1894, the journals served as both diary and sketchbook, capturing Vuillard's thoughts in word and image. The journals are difficult to read and to translate not only because of Vuillard's tiny, erratic scrawl but also because the entries are neither punctuated nor written in complete sentences, often omitting key words and dates.

Vuillard began keeping a journal in 1888, when he was twenty; the first dated entry is from 20 November of that year. Although he kept a journal for fifty-two years, he was for the first two decades a sporadic diarist, beginning to make daily entries only after 1907. The first two volumes cover a span of seventeen years. Little written commentary appears in the first notebook, devoted to the years 1888 to 1890, but the second notebook reveals a great deal about Vuillard's thoughts from 1890 to 1905, a crucial period of his development. That these journals were of great signifi-cance to Vuillard throughout his life is clear from evidence that he reread and annotated all the volumes at a later date. Years after making his original entries, for example, he inserted chronological lists of major commissions or exhibitions into the journals as a kind of autobiographical gloss (see Appendix A). The care and, perhaps, obsessiveness with which Vuillard reviewed his journals is suggested by the fact that in the later volumes he went through and underlined in red pencil all references to his mother and in blue pencil all references to his current projects. Curiously, he wrote down his thoughts, feelings, and observations in pencil instead of ink and left his daily activities unremarked. But in spite of abundant evidence that Vuillard often reexamined and consulted these early journals, the later volumes shed relatively little light on the early years.

The young artist evidently carried the pocket-sized carnets with him wherever he went. The entries for the early years indicate, however, that Vuillard would write and draw in them daily for as long a period as a month and then leave the book untouched for as much as a year. As a consequence, the contents of the early journals are varied: mathematical equations and anatomical drawings reflect what Vuillard was learning in school, while whimsical observations of the world around him—from people on the street, in the parks, and at the theater to landscape vignettes of electric light illuminating trees—reveal a tendency toward caricature and humor that was seldom manifested in his more formal painted works.

At the same time that Vuillard was recording his feelings in the journals, he was giving his personality pictorial form in a series of self-portraits. One of these, dating from 1888–89 (fig. 2), shows Vuillard in a three-quarter view with his face in shadow and his neck and shoulders shrouded in a dark jacket. A warm, whitish-yellow curtain that hangs behind him in vertical folds creates a stark contrast to the darkness of his face: light barely touches Vuillard's nose and forehead, while it bathes the curtain behind him. His features are difficult to decipher. Vuillard's introspective nature is suggested by the fuzzy, shadowy quality of the work. He nonetheless relieves the somber palette by painting his ear with highlights of a bright, pure red. The small scale of the work and the monochrome palette of browns show the influence of the old masters Vuillard was studying at that time in the Louvre.

Between 1888 and 1890 Vuillard looked more to the traditional still lifes of the eighteenth-century painter Jean-Baptiste-Siméon Chardin and his nineteenth-century follower Henri Fantin-Latour, together with other old master paintings in the Louvre, than to his immediate Impressionist predecessors or to his older contemporaries Gauguin, Seurat, and Vincent van Gogh. The importance of old master painting to Vuillard's developing artistic sensibility is evident throughout the first volume of his journal, and his earliest paintings must be seen in light of his frequent visits to the Louvre (see Appendix B). Toward the end of 1888 Vuillard comments in his journals on the Northern masters Hans Holbein, Lucas Cranach, Adriaen van Ostade, Rembrandt van Rijn, Hans Memling, and Gerard Dou and on the French painters Chardin, Jean-Auguste-Dominique Ingres, and Camille Corot.

Because none of the self-portraits is dated, we can judge their chronology only on the basis of stylistic evolution. Another Vuillard *Self-portrait* (fig. 3), probably painted at about the same time, reveals a much livelier palette than the first. We know from accounts of his friends that Vuillard had a reddish beard, and in this picture the whole palette is composed of warm, reddish tones. Where in the earlier picture his features were indistinct and difficult to decipher from the shadows, in this work the eyes and the outline of his nose are clearly defined. A white shirt collar alleviates the somberness of his attire. Although this painting is warmer and brighter in tone and more specific in detail, Vuillard nonetheless carried over from the earlier picture the red highlight in the ear.

The principal characteristic that distinguishes this painting is the horizontal divider in the foreground space that Vuillard used to distance himself from the picture plane. It is difficult to determine exactly what this dividing object is until one examines another painting that defines the same object more clearly. *Self-portrait in a Mirror* (fig. 4) reveals the horizontal object as the bamboo frame of a mirror, and the vague putty-colored pattern below it as wallpaper. This pictorial obfuscation becomes a more firmly implanted characteristic of Vuillard's art by the 1890s. In his paintings of those years, in fact, objects are often blurred or foreshortened beyond recognition, so that only comparison of a group of paintings yields understanding of a motif. Such comparisons not only help identify objects that are unclear in one painting but also

Self-portrait

1888–89

oil on cardboard, 10¼ x 7½ inches,

private collection, New York

give the viewer a sense of the way Vuillard used a limited repertory of objects in his paintings, reconfiguring them each time.

Vuillard's face, reflected in the bamboo-framed mirror, is every bit as fuzzy as it is in the earliest portrait, which suggests that these three pictures were painted relatively close in time. But in *Self-portrait in a Mirror,* Vuillard has introduced two kinds of focus. His features in this later painting are indistinct because his focus on

3 🙟

Self-portrait

c. 1891

oil on board laid on cradled panel, 10¾ x

8⅜ *inches, private collection,*

Switzerland

the mirror frame is absolutely clear: he thus gives painted form to a phenomenon of vision, the eye's inability to focus on two planes at one time.

 The mirror, which is hinted at in one painting and made fully explicit only in another, points directly to the inherent paradox of the self-portrait: the impossibility of truly apprehending oneself. A person can never perceive himself by direct vision: a mirror must stand between the painting subject and the painted object, creating a distance between a person's appearance to others and the reverse image that he actually is able to see.

12

4

Self-portrait in a Mirror

1888–90

oil on canvas, $17\frac{1}{2}$ x $21\frac{1}{8}$ inches,

Mr. Lew Wasserman, Beverly Hills,

California

More than the earlier of the portraits, *Self-portrait in a Mirror* is a painting in a long tradition of images that explore this inescapable paradox. Vuillard's focus on the mirror instead of on his own image only compounds the irony of his commentary. Yet the subtle details of composition and facture that enliven the preceding two pictures are also present here. The bamboo frame is shown hanging on a patterned wallpaper, but the upper left corner of the frame is omitted, disrupting the symmetry of the picture. In a further attempt to relieve the regularity of the composition, Vuillard cut off the bamboo frame with two unidentifiable patterned strips in the lowest section of the canvas.

In contrast to the patterned border of the composition, the reflected image is blurred and painted in simple monochrome green for the back wall and ceiling, and in white for the skylight, the door or wall beyond, and Vuillard's smock. As in the border, the mirror space is made dynamic by subtle disruptions of logic and regularity. The wall or door on the right recedes at a sharp angle, while the skylight above Vuillard's head seems to operate on an entirely different system and slopes sharply downward. Although Vuillard situated himself virtually in the center of this composition, inconsistencies of scale and perspective preclude an understanding of how the actual space unfolds. The juxtaposition of flat pattern and complicated spatial recession seen in this early self-portrait constitutes a device that Vuillard played with throughout his career.

About 1890, when he painted *Self-portrait in a Mirror*, Vuillard began to assume a more distant point of view and to introduce into his work a complex commentary on his craft, including here specific allusions to his profession: the skylight of the studio, the painter's smock, and the mirror frame, which forms an interior "picture" framing his own image. A year earlier Vuillard had painted a rather large double portrait of himself and his friend Waroquy (fig. 1).[3] He depicted both of them in

13

nearly full figure, painting the entire picture in tones of green and brown. For the first and only time, Vuillard unequivocally showed himself in the act of painting; he holds a palette and several brushes in his hand with more brushes visible in a vase behind him. He continued in this painting to portray himself in virtual monochrome, with half his face in dark shadow. His friend Waroquy is portrayed almost completely out of focus—much more summarily painted than Vuillard himself.

The mirror in which Vuillard and his friend are reflected is hinted at so obliquely as almost to go unnoticed: only a bottle, placed unobtrusively in the lower right foreground, indicates that the entire image is a reflection. The bottle and its mirror image are more brightly colored and more clearly depicted than anything else in the canvas. The greenish tone that bathes the rest of the picture seems to be cast by the looking glass itself.

Vuillard appears to have left several sections of the canvas unfinished, especially the area where Waroquy stands. Vuillard's own left leg, which emerges from the obscure middle ground, appears thin and awkward, all the more so because Vuillard did not indicate his right leg at all. Yet his hand, which reaches for a brush, is painted with greater clarity than any other part of either figure, indicating Vuillard's continued emphasis on his craft.

Waroquy, about whom almost nothing is known, was apparently a close friend of the artist in the late 1880s and early 1890s. We do not know his first name, although his surname appears often in Vuillard's journals.[4] Yet Vuillard chose to portray him casually, his face out of focus and his body indistinct. Although the forms of the two men seem to merge together, the differentiation of focus emphasizes their separateness. The shift from the extreme clarity of the bottles and Vuillard's hand, to the shadowy figure Vuillard cast for himself, to the complete blur in which he painted his friend is an effect that Vuillard would exaggerate to even greater degree in later years. The size of this work marks it as an important effort in Vuillard's early career, and the several references to the work that appear in the journals indicate the importance of this double portrait to the young painter. In a brief outline of his life from 1888 until 1904, Vuillard listed the portrait of Waroquy as one of only four important events occurring in 1889.[5]

Another double portrait, *Self-portrait with Sister* (fig. 5), depicts the painter embracing his beloved sister Marie, whom he called Mimi and who was to marry his best friend, the painter Ker-Xavier Roussel, in 1893. The painting represents a different approach to the genre in both style and technique. Probably painted circa 1892, about two years after the *Portrait of Vuillard and Waroquy*, this painting is a study in contrasts. Vuillard's style has changed completely to one where flat shapes of unmodulated color define the forms. The figures appear to have merged, their faces and bodies so close together that they allow no space between or around them. The top of Vuillard's head extends beyond the canvas, and his hands are depicted at either side of the picture on a scale just bigger than the canvas. His image is thus slightly larger than the canvas itself, lending a certain monumentality to his form in what is,

Self-portrait with Sister

c. 1892

oil on canvas, 9 x 6½ inches,

The Philadelphia Museum of Art;

The Louis E. Stern Collection

in fact, a very small picture. Pentimenti show that he wanted his own image to be larger than that of his sister, and that he reworked the outline of her head to make her appear smaller. Vuillard's sister is seen from behind, defined only by her hair gathered at her neck. Her only visible feature, the simple rounded outline of her cheek, suggests that Vuillard is embracing a woman much younger than himself, when, in fact, his sister was seven years his senior.[6] This is an image both compelling and disturbing, depicting as it does an intimacy almost too intense for a brother and sister to share, and it differs significantly from the more typical pictures of Marie sewing or working in her mother's atelier.

Stylistically, the *Self-portrait with Sister* represents a radical departure from the rather traditional images of the late 1880s and predicts the path Vuillard's art would take in the last decade of the century. The simple forms, unrelieved by shadows or modeling, and the flat areas of color inscribed by thin outlines are very different from the molded, shadowy forms of the earlier self-portraits. This stylistic change is foreshadowed in Vuillard's journal. The entries from late 1890 show the month-by-month movement of the artist's theoretical concerns away from Naturalism and toward a Symbolist aesthetic. The dramatic change in Vuillard's theory must be seen in light of two major events: Paul Sérusier's return from Brittany in 1888 with *The Talisman*, a small landscape he had painted under the direction of Gauguin, and Maurice Denis's publication in August 1890 of the "Définition du néo-traditionnisme."

Sérusier used his painting to illustrate to his friends the dramatic revelation he had experienced while painting with Gauguin, who had encouraged him to paint a tree yellow and the earth red, thus transforming nature by the exercise of his intellect and imagination.[7] Sérusier urged the Nabis to take Gauguin's advice to choose colors free from the constraints of traditional academic depictions of nature and to intensify colors seen in nature beyond the limits that the Impressionists had reached.

In 1888, however, Vuillard was still searching for a pictorial harmony in nature itself that could be reproduced on the canvas. As he wrote,

> We perceive nature through the senses, which give us the images of forms and of colors, or sound, etc. A form, a color, exists only in relation to another . . .[8]

Although Sérusier's interaction with the Nabis took place in 1888, his theories did not affect Vuillard's art until later; in fact Vuillard identified "l'année de Sérusier" (the year of Sérusier) as 1890 in the two chronologies of his life. In 1888–89 Vuillard continued to make daily trips to the Louvre to study the old masters, whose influence we still see in his art at this time. The only suggestion of a departure from conventional modes of representation in these early works is the accent of red that Vuillard added to his ear in his earliest self-portraits (figs. 2 and 3). But Vuillard could have learned this device from Corot as easily as from Gauguin:

> Corot, an accent in some hazy thing, in a perfect harmony of a number of grays a sound. (with respect to a pastel study in light gray, two pure tones, one red the other green . . . thus the pictures of *corot* are always but a symphony of grays with one single differing tone.[9]

Only in 1890, when Vuillard added to Sérusier's advice the lesson he learned from Denis's treatise, did his art change dramatically. The "Définition du néo-traditionnisme" begins with the statement that has now come to stand for the whole Nabi movement: that a painting, "before it is a battlehorse, a nude woman, or some anecdote—is essentially a flat surface covered with colors in a certain order."[10] In late August 1890, just after Denis's work had been published, Vuillard wrote that he wanted

> to conceive a picture as a series of accords, distancing oneself definitively from the Naturalist idea.[11]

The "series of accords" clearly is taken directly from Denis's idea of colors and forms arranged "in a certain order," and his friend's encouragement was also probably at the root of Vuillard's own desire to distance himself from the Naturalism that he previously had sought.

One week later in early September, Vuillard wrote again about the expression of a work of art coming directly from its inherent formal qualities:

> Expression *pure and simple* coming purely and simply from the lines and colors of the thing itself . . . Why, of course—from painting and not from associated ideas.[12]

Here Vuillard is as close to Denis's theory as he will ever get. By 1890 Denis and Vuillard had been companions for at least six years, and the potency of Denis's thoughts no doubt was increased by the friendship of the two artists. They were at the Lycée Condorcet together in 1884, and their connection continued at the Ecole des Beaux-Arts and through their participation in the Nabi group.

Nevertheless, Vuillard continually felt the need to distinguish his own art, indeed the very process of making art, from the achievements of his young and innovative friends. Again and again in his diaries he probed his feelings about the flood of ideas coming from other members of the Nabis—painters who, like Denis, were sometimes more adept than he at articulating their theories. The scope of Vuillard's inquiry is evident from a passage in his journal written shortly after the publication of Denis's "Définition":

> Thus objective expression is the only thing that matters . . . the expression of lines and shapes (don't attempt to imagine the subjective expression of lines and shapes) . . . From there . . . renunciation to a definitive, immediate work (we are not after all primitives!) but calm and beauty of the spirit of Sérusier!) . . . maybe quickly if I have the courage to apply these ideas![13]

These jotted notes seem to reflect what must have been Vuillard's deep confusion and inner misgivings about the repercussions these ideas would have on his painting, at that time still deeply rooted in the style and subject matter of the old masters. Vuillard hovered between defending objective expression, naive and yet forceful in its immediacy, and recognizing the subjective power of lines and shapes. "We are not primitives!" he declared, as if to fend off not only the radical new ideas of Denis, Sérusier, and by extension Gauguin, but also their crude, primitivising style. He admired Sérusier, whom he felt had been able not only to keep these difficult issues

17

under control but also to apply these ideas to his painting.[14] To resolve his inner struggle, Vuillard attempted to apply these powerful new ideas to the old masters, ascribing the affective beauty of such works not to their verisimilitude but to the abstract qualities revealed by the harmony of their color and line. He wrote, for example, of the still lifes of Chardin, which

> . . . give pleasure through the agreement of tones and the outward design and not by the greater or lesser exactitude with which they recall their models, unknown to us. Difficulty of really getting this into my head after the long hours spent two years ago in front of these canvases filled with naturalist ideas, not understanding that between those ideas of copying of that time and the pure and simple pleasures of these harmonies of tone, there was no relationship at all . . . Nothing is important save the spiritual state one is in to be able to subjectify his thought to a sensation [and] to think only of the sensation all the while searching the means of expression.[15]

Chardin was an artist to whom Vuillard referred throughout his life, although for different reasons at each stage. Although toward the end of Vuillard's career Chardin was to loom large in terms of the particularly French qualities of his painting, at this early crucial point in his life, he looked to Chardin for the harmony of his palette and the shapes on the canvas, regardless of how faithful to the model. This formalism is a direct application of Denis's definition of painting as a "surface covered with colors assembled in a certain order." But where Denis intended this as a prescription for future art, Vuillard tried to understand these qualities as eternal and universal attributes.

Vuillard was, in fact, aware of this distinction between his artistic point of view and that of his friend Denis. The passage in which he discusses Chardin continues with a reflection on Denis:

> The amazing impression of Denis's drawings; the great wisdom will be when I shall see these works without reference to myself, and immediate comparison; any other expression I might convey . . . I've just done a fresh young woman, running, in the Prud'honnesque lines that Denis can't match; but what I lack is the assurance and the continuous working that is his consciousness.[16]

Vuillard's uneasy preoccupation with judging himself in relation to his peers, while undoubtedly the ordinary consequence of starting a career, was a focal element in his journals and letters during the 1890s. Self-doubt was to remain with him, a constant theme in his writings even as he reached his maturity and became one of the prominent painters in his circle. Self-doubt led him to strive for critical objectivity. In a journal entry from 1890 he admonished himself:

> Think about the effect produced by others' works; one has to look at these works [one's own works] like those of others in order to get an impression of them, and to judge their expression.[17]

In March 1891 Vuillard was still sorting out the lesson of Denis. He began to explore the emotional potential of colors and forms on a canvas, the subjective power of the art of the past, and the emotional force latent even in an *académie,* an academic life study that was a routine exercise for students at the Ecole de Beaux-Arts.

> I want to do one . . . with an old *académie.* Why: In leafing through these old studies I was struck by the expression of a few rare ones among them that hadn't been too ruined by caring [too much] about rendering the different parts of the object represented. . . . first of all, to use the words of the past the *académie* in question is more than an ensemble, in other words it forms a *whole;* thus all the elements employed are harmonious to the whole . . . (since I no longer consider them as *details,* a detail being *part* of a whole and in art the harmonious part of a whole) so the ensemble is no longer an ensemble, it is a sheet of paper covered with a lot of disparate elements; that is to say, each having a different expression, the ensemble cannot have a powerful [expression]. Thus there's no use saying in front of this *académie,* in order to make a painting out of it, I'm going to make an Ingres, or a Delacroix, or a Rembrandt. . . . let us move on to the emotion that it gives to me, the lines or the strokes that I put on a canvas will be mine. [18]

Vuillard believed that the power of a work of art came from its "expression," which changed according to the individual. "The subject of *any* work," he wrote, "is an emotion simple and natural to the author."[19] Thus, even in a particular *académie,* Vuillard could find a powerful, individual, emotional truth revealed. Concerned with applying Denis's or Sérusier's theories to his paintings, Vuillard admitted to himself that between his own emotions and the actual work there was a direct, immediate connection.

By the next month Vuillard had strengthened his convictions. While still feeling the need to respond to Denis, Vuillard apparently had acquired more faith in himself when he wrote in April 1891:

> Pure and simple observation is a *deed,* a simple act of life, and it is this simple and primitive observation that is necessary, that *is.* If therefore we were simple beings, and not . . . spoiled by prejudices and habits, our works would be easily beautiful because there would be no struggle to distinguish the truth from falsehood. Thus in front of a work of art one shouldn't ask if such and such a theory is applied, but is it beautiful? All the same, we speak of a beautiful color a beautiful line, and yes you experience a moment of emotion over this color or that line that synthesizes All in that moment. Now a picture for example isn't this color or that form, it is the sum of these colors or of those forms.[20]

This quotation represents in the microcosm of a private monologue the public debate Vuillard conducted with his peers. At the center of the debate was the distinction between direct observation and the application of theory to painting. Vuillard believed for himself that observation was direct, a "simple act of life." He stated that the sensation of beauty depended upon an emotion imparted by certain colors and lines, concluding that a work of art will be beautiful if there is a direct connection between what is observed, "what is," and what is depicted by the arrangement of colors and lines on the canvas. Vuillard's "beautiful" resulted from unprejudicial observation or the naive eye, which avoids the struggle between truth and falsehood because it is

19

direct. To Vuillard, the inherent integrity of this connection was more important than the application of any theory. In this way he distinguished himself from Denis and Sérusier, whose interest in the symbolic role of form and color led them to paint from theories rather than from direct observation:

> It's necessary to take his [Sérusier's] theories only as theories and not as his way of applying them; in this way when he draws lines . . . he knows what theoretical idea he is obeying; one mustn't imitate him in dreaming of the single expression that his work conveys.[21]

Vuillard continued to struggle with his own perceptions and ideas about painting. As his thoughts remained in a state of flux, even as late as 1894, he had trouble asserting his own individuality:

> In painting isn't it all the same the evocation of these interior images by means that are likewise very general, colors and forms. Art consists of introducing an order into these means suggestive of these images.[22]

It is interesting to recall once again Denis's famous statement because it differs from Vuillard's thoughts in a significant way. Denis, in his "Définition," had implied that before a painting took on its subject matter it was essentially a surface covered with colors assembled in a certain order. Vuillard, albeit four years later, took almost an opposite approach. He treated the images as primary and the order in which the artist distilled them as secondary.

In short, Denis worked from his theory about the arrangement of color and line, while Vuillard concerned himself with such arrangements only after his direct connection with his subject. In this respect, Vuillard had not changed his approach from the one he expressed while he contemplated Chardin. Although the words Vuillard used reflect those of his friend, his art had a fundamentally different point of departure.

The outcome of Vuillard's theoretical struggle can best be seen in two self-portraits from 1891–92, extraordinarily compelling works of Vuillard's Nabi style (figs. 6 and 7). The two compositions are strikingly similar. In each the painter faces to the left, with his eyes cocked back to look directly at the viewer. The quizzical glance and shadowed expression of the earlier self-portraits is gone, and a new forthright gaze reflects Vuillard's increasing confidence as a painter. The two works clearly date from the same time, but the octagonal work appears to be the later version since the background is less sketchy and the few awkward passages of the other picture have been resolved.[23] In these paintings Vuillard reached the pinnacle of his Nabi achievement. Vuillard's face is composed of flat planes of solid color, as Maurice Denis prescribed, and these abstract, sinuous shapes represent in the brilliance of their colors the freedom of imagination that Sérusier encouraged his Nabi friends to explore.

From a close comparison of the two portraits, the viewer can reconstruct a series of problems and their solutions. In the rectangular picture (fig. 6), Vuillard seemed unable to resolve the transition around the ear from the face to the neck. He created a more solid and sinuous outline in the octagonal work (fig. 7), where his bright yellow hair joins his orange beard in the form of a sideburn, completely encircling the face. Where in the earlier painting the brown shadow on his forehead takes a complex curving form much like the shadow on his face, Vuillard simplified the outlines in the octagonal panel and gave the articulated shadow on the face full attention. In the earlier work Vuillard wears a blue jacket and a white shirt against a green background. He simplified the color scheme in the final version by adding yellow to the shirt so that it harmonizes with his hair and by blending the tone of the shadows and the background. The change in the panel's shape also signals a resolution: the octagonal format not only frames the face but also lends a dynamism to Vuillard's slightly off-center pose.

Vuillard showered the green/brown background of the octagonal portrait with a complement of red dots. Vuillard's dots tend to float on the top surface of the picture plane, contrasting with the flat forms that make up the rest of the design. This effect distinguishes Vuillard's use of these Neo-Impressionist devices from that of Seurat or van Gogh, who seem to be the artist's most obvious models. In Seurat's works, of course, dots usually cover the entire painting and create a sense of vibration throughout the canvas. Van Gogh manipulates dots to great effect in his self-portraits, creating halos around his head with a celestial shower of pattern.[24] (Although he mentioned neither Seurat nor van Gogh in his journals, Vuillard might have seen some of their pictures in Paris at the Salon des Indépendants in 1890.) In Vuillard's octagonal self-portrait, however, the dots form neither a halo nor an optical vibration, but they create a spatial ambiguity in the juxtaposition of flat areas against patterned ones that he was to explore throughout the decade.

Of all Vuillard's self-portraits, these two are the most potent. No longer distanced by the deliberate inclusion of a mirror, with a frame to contribute a sense of artifice and calculation, these Nabi self-portraits are vibrantly direct. Their utter lack of detail, which mutes their actual resemblance to the painter, allows them to soar beyond the particularities of likeness to the artist's spiritual essence. It is as if, through his adoption of the Symbolist aesthetic, Vuillard had discovered a way out of the paradox of the mirror. He had found the key to the world beyond representation. Vuillard addresses this very thought in his journal:

> A thing remarkable in museums and in the history of painting, the more mystic painters are the more vivid their colors (reds blues yellows) . . .[25]

It is also true that the further the image departs from the specific depiction of the physiognomy—the closer it comes to the pure language of form and color—the more powerful a symbol it becomes. For the rest of the decade, Vuillard was to avoid concentrating on his own image, exploring instead the powerful symbolism of the interior.

6 ❧

Self-portrait

1891–92

oil on cardboard, 14⅛ x 11¼ inches,

private collection, Los Angeles, photo

© Douglas M. Parker

7

Self-portrait

1892

oil on cardboard, 14¼ x 11 inches

(octagonal), private collection, Paris

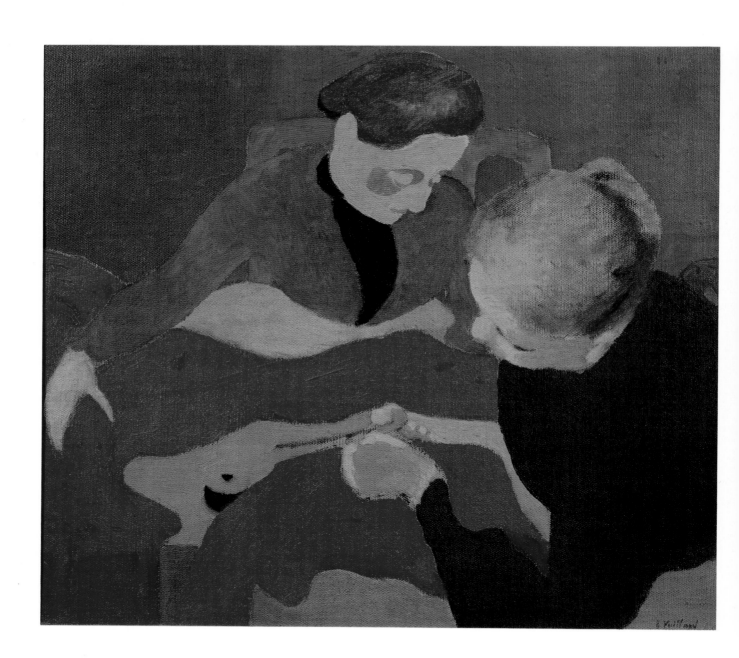

ICONS OF INWARDNESS:

THE SEWING PAINTINGS

. . . I have never lived except with women in those places from which I

took my subjects . . .

EV I.2, 47 (27 July 1894)

8 ❧

The Dressmakers

1891

oil on canvas, 18¾ x 21⅝ inches,

Josefowitz Collection

25

As early as November 1888 Vuillard filled a page of his journal with scenes of women working by lamplight around a table (see fig. 39). Although these images were not transformed into paintings until a few years later, they nonetheless were a compelling subject for him from the time he began to think of himself as an artist. It is perhaps no coincidence that on the same journal page Vuillard made reference to the works in the Louvre of Jan Steen and Chardin and included a sketch of a painting by Jan Vermeer. The intimate and sometimes disturbing depictions of daily life that characterize the works of these Dutch masters and the quiet power of Chardin's images of governesses and serving maids form the art historical background to Vuillard's scenes of women at work in his mother's atelier. Vuillard was to paint these scenes throughout the 1890s, when his mother's corset business dominated the daily activities of the household.

Vuillard, however, was grappling in the early 1890s with how to reconcile such quotidian subject matter to a new-found Symbolist aesthetic. In his paintings of seamstresses, he adapted that aesthetic to the world around him. For all their earthiness and concern for telling detail, these paintings transcend the merely worka-day to a realm of emotional truth that is beyond specific time and place. Indeed, in spite of documentary qualities, these paintings must be read and understood as an ongoing interior monologue: no one work can be fully deciphered without reference to the others. The seamstress paintings are a series of scenes, impinging on and borrowing from one another.

The central character in many of these works, such as *Woman Mending* (fig. 10), is Marie Justine Alexandrine Michaud Vuillard, the painter's mother, whom he called his muse. Whether she is shown at work, as here, or at rest, as in *Madame Vuillard in Profile* (fig. 9), the paintings pay homage to her and to her profession; they are lyrical tributes to the subject of women at work.

Much has been written about Vuillard's relationship with his mother since they lived together until she died in 1928 when the artist was sixty years old. To understand fully Vuillard's work, it is necessary to explore his mother's professional life. The prolific surface patterning of his canvases clearly is rooted in the abundance of materials he saw around the house, which served as the workshop of his mother's corset business; the decision to paint scenes of women sewing also must have been occasioned by the everyday activities of the household.

Contrary to what most scholars have written, Mme. Vuillard was a corsetmaker, not a dressmaker.[1] This long-established misunderstanding has spawned significant confusion about the family's social standing. In the commercial directory, or *Bottin,* of the 1880s and 1890s, several different categories were listed under corsets: *corsets en gros* (wholesale), *corsets sans couture, corsets,* and *fournitures pour corsets.* Mme. Vuillard was listed under the general category of corsets rather than the listing for those who made corsets without doing any dressmaking, so it can be assumed that some part of Mme. Vuillard's business was dedicated to couture. Her son's paintings of the atelier, in fact, show women handling the kind of cloth that dresses were made of, and

26

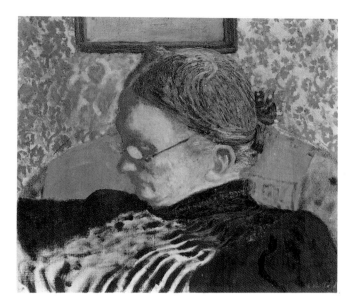

9 ❧

Madame Vuillard in Profile

1898

oil on canvas, 13 x 14⅞ inches, collection

of Mrs. John Hay Whitney, New York

10 ❧

Woman Mending

1891–92

oil on cardboard, 11¼ x 9¼ inches

(oval), Josefowitz Collection

lengths of cloth that suggest the making of outer- rather than underwear. Nonetheless, Mme. Vuillard was never listed in the professional directory as anything but a *corsetière*.

Even the printed form letter announcing the purchase of her business makes clear Mme. Vuillard's professional ties. The letter, headed with the date "le _____ 187__," stated that Mme. Vuillard had taken over the corset-making business of one Mme. Duval-Caron, located at 60, rue Neuve St.-Augustin, and assured the recipient that should she continue to patronize the company, Mme. Vuillard would put herself entirely at the customer's service.[2]

This letter reveals other information that until now has escaped the notice of historians. The usual assumption has been that Mme. Vuillard opened her business when her husband died in 1884.[3] Yet the date on the printed letter—le _____ 187__—indicates that Mme. Vuillard was in business for herself at least before 1880. An unpublished letter in the Vuillard family archives to Mme. Vuillard from Mme. Duval-Caron indicates that in mid-March 1878 the business arrangement was coming to a close. "We will see," Mme. Duval-Caron wrote, "whether, as you say, we can in the end come to an understanding."[4] Mme. Vuillard's name first appears in the commercial *Bottin* of 1879, perhaps indicating that the beginning date of her new business was late 1878 (thus the desire for leaving blank the last digit of the date on her announcement). Mme. Vuillard not only purchased the business from Mme.

Duval-Caron, but also took over the apartment where she had lived and worked. The fact that Mme. Vuillard was at work a full six years before her husband's death, from the time that Vuillard was eleven years old, means that Vuillard grew up surrounded by women at work.

The corset business in France was highly structured and had been so since 1675 when a royal edict prohibiting couturières from making corsets established two distinct professions. That same year the king had decreed that people must be outfitted in clothing by those of their own sex. As a result, couturières were forbidden to hire tailors to sew for them, just as master tailors were prohibited from employing seamstresses. It was at this point that the corset trade per se was born, its workers taking the title *tailleurs de corps de femmes et d'enfants.* In spite of these elaborate restrictions, women corsetmakers essentially decorated the garment while the tailor was responsible for its construction.[5]

The corset trade thrived late in the 1820s and 1830s; before 1828 only two patents were registered relating to the corset, but between 1828 and 1848 there were sixty-four.[6] The corset trade expanded with the appearance of sewing machines and, like other industries, with the increasing speed of transport that broadened the market through sales to tourists and for export.[7] In 1878, a *chambre syndicale* was founded, consisting of five *comités,* each having to do with an aspect of corset production: *corsets en gros, corsetières sur mesure, fabricants de busc et de ressorts, fabricants de baleines et de cornes,* and *fabricants de tissus et de fournitures diverses.*[8]

In the related couture business, a clear-cut hierarchy existed. The *petite couturière* worked at home with one or two apprentices. Her clients, from *la petite bourgeoisie* or *dans le peuple,* would supply the material and expect the *patronne* herself to sew the dress for a small fee. The *moyenne couturière,* usually a woman, would furnish the material for the clothes; the client chose the fabrics and decided from a magazine on the style of the garment. *Grand couture* was on a completely different scale in that the house was run by a man and the styles were unique to the establishment, its place of business as luxurious as its clientele.[9]

The corset business was probably analogous to that of the *petite* and *moyenne couture.* Yet some corsetmakers had establishments of a scale that could link them to the higher levels of the couture trade. The Maison Léoty, for example, not only participated in extravagant advertising but also had an extensive collection of corsets spanning the centuries; Ernest Léoty, its proprietor, published the definitive book on the history of the corset in 1893.[10]

If we assume a similar hierarchy in the corset trade, Mme. Vuillard certainly fell into the lower range of the profession. Because no documents have survived from her years as a corsetmaker, however, it is difficult to establish her rank definitively. She left neither a will nor an *inventaire après décès,* indicating that at the time of her death Vuillard was already in control of her possessions and that she did not have much to bequeath.[11] Yet, from Vuillard's paintings and from the contemporary accounts of his friends, we know that she had at least two assistants. The corset industry, furthermore, was at its peak during the last decade of the nineteenth century. Despite the tremendous privations suffered by those who worked in the industry, figures from the *Ministère du travail et de la prévoyance sociale* indicate that the output of lingerie in general in 1890, when Mme. Vuillard's business was in full swing, was almost double what it would be in 1905.[12]

It is not known whether Mme. Vuillard was politically active as a working woman. Yet one very interesting piece of information exists that might connect Mme. Vuillard to a larger movement that sought to improve the plight of the working woman in the clothing industry. In 1892 a group of workers in the clothing business, including *couturières, modistes, corsetières, brodistes, plumassières,* banded together to create the only union of the trade, which took the name L'Aiguillée, a name given to an 1893 painting by Vuillard (see fig. 24). By 1897 there were 1,395 union members[13] who could count on the syndicate for a variety of services including "the material advantages of corporative institutions, placement offices, legal departments, information services, a fund for interest-free loans, a fund for the encouragement of mutual aid societies, a home for workers separated from their families, [and] free medical care."[14] In 1897, when Leon de Seilhac wrote his book on the clothing industry, the headquarters of L'Aiguillée were located at 342, rue St. Honoré, the very building in which Mme. Vuillard lived and ran her business in that year.

Mme. Vuillard's corset-making atelier was the focus of activity in the Vuillard household from at least 1879, when Edouard was eleven years old, until 1898, when his mother retired and he took over the responsibility for her support. These years span Vuillard's youth, adolescence, and early days as a student of painting right through his mature years as a Nabi. His paintings of seamstresses depict women sewing alone, in pairs, and in groups in the atelier. Even though these pictures relate to his mother's atelier, the specific identity of the seamstresses is rarely clear. Certain figures can be identified as Mme. Vuillard or Marie, but Vuillard seems to focus more on the work they do than on the personalities of the sitters—and even so, he never identifies specifically the objects the women are sewing.

Paintings of isolated women in the atelier often show them in postures of self-absorption. A small painting of Marie Vuillard, *The Seamstress (The Servant),* circa 1891 (fig. 11), depicts her hunched over a table, her hands resting on its edge. Seen from the waist up, she stands out as the vertical element in an otherwise horizontal composition, with bands of paint to represent a table covered with fabric, a banquette, and wallpaper. The painting is remarkably sophisticated in its visual organization, particularly in light of its tiny size. With its loose pattern and green/ochre tone, the table visually echoes the wallpaper behind the figure, while the solid red and black of the banquette offsets the figure's print dress of black and light orange. Her face and hands are distinguished by their lack of pattern, while her hair becomes a decorative design in which alternating stripes of dark and light indicate shadows and highlights. The outline of the face is not unlike the caricatures Vuillard drew incessantly in his journals, and it gives a sprightliness to the composition in keeping

29

with the feeling created by the many patterns.[15] The color of the face repeats a similar tone in the material on the table and completes the visual circle formed by the hunched shoulders. The wallpaper's green background with dark green, red, and orange highlights unifies the picture by bringing all of its colors into the wallpaper's floral motif.

Vuillard compounded the visual play of flattened planes by setting an enigmatic square of black in the lower left portion of the composition so that it appears to rest virtually on the frame. This black square, outlined on two sides by red, parallels the picture frame and makes little pretense at referring to a specific object, although it might be read as a small box. Its color duplicates the horizontal strip of black and red that constitutes the banquette or dado behind the figure, reiterating its flatness.

Another striking feature of the composition is the area Vuillard chose to leave unpainted. Often in Vuillard's compositions major parts of the work were left untouched by paint, sometimes constituting solid elements of the work and other times forming parts of the background. At the lower center of this picture, an area of unpainted cardboard forms a sinuous shape where the figure's torso meets the table. The hair is also basically unpainted cardboard with highlights and shadows added, and the background color of the tablecloth is unpainted cardboard as well. The central unpainted area appears to come forward because it is light in color and unpatterned, in marked contrast to the other elements in the composition. But it also can be read as a hole in the center of the picture that leaves the raw support clearly visible.[16] This unpainted element causes the spatial configuration to become even more complex than the layering of patterns would indicate, and the meaning of the picture grows evasive.

In the painting *Girl by the Door* (fig. 12), dated 1891, the figure is wearing a similarly patterned dress, the entire background of which is unpainted cardboard. The hunched pose indicates that this figure is Vuillard's sister Marie; she is often depicted in this submissive posture in other works from the 1890s. Although her figure is bent over, just fitting into the composition, the severe black line of the dress and the unpainted background flatten out her form, making her almost seem to merge with the door behind her.

This deliberate avoidance of representational clarity and an apparent love for spatial ambiguity can also be seen in Vuillard's prints of the 1890s, such as *La Couturière (The Seamstress)* (fig. 13), in which the artist manipulates a tightly knit group of decorative motifs. Here, as in *The Seamstress (The Servant),* patterned areas are offset by isolated sections of flat color, but even these have been cajoled by Vuillard into a decorative role. The sinuous contours of the material extending all the way across the composition take on a role as decorative as the woman's dress and the wallpaper behind her. Rather than adding highlights and shadows to give the material a tactile three-dimensionality, Vuillard simply added four curving lines with patterns that stand out against the solid background of the material and give it form. The woman's face is attenuated and whimsical, recalling the woman in *The Seamstress (The Servant)*

11 ❧

The Seamstress (The Servant)

1891

oil on cardboard, 7¹/₈ x 9¹/₈ inches, private

collection, New York

12 ❧

Girl by the Door

1891

oil on cardboard, 11¹/₂ x 8 inches, private

collection, New York

The patterns in this composition are contained within clearly defined areas: the top section of the door and the window frames, whose insets feature a zigzag design in pale green ink, and the wallpaper whose background picks up the light green tone yet again. The wallpaper pattern, probably applied by hand with a wood block, also picks up the zigzag from above, this time in a darker green.[17] Although the surface appears lively in its contrast of details, the lithograph actually consists of only four shades of green—a pale wash for the background, dark olive in the wallpaper pattern, bright green on the dress, and the lighter wash on its collar—and one tone of gray, which Vuillard used to outline the figure and the features of the room and to describe the material.

An ink drawing of the composition (fig. 14) shows how Vuillard worked out the final details to achieve a harmonious composition. The principal difference between the two compositions is that the windows shown at the upper margin in the drawing are rendered as a series of dots and the wallpaper behind the figure shows flowers over a diamond pattern. In the lithograph, Vuillard reduced both design elements to zigzags, creating a greater compositional harmony. Although the figure wears a checked dress in both drawing and print, its pattern is subtly different in each work, appearing as a windowpane plaid in the print and as a pattern of aligned squares in the drawing.

Vuillard continued throughout the 1890s to manipulate patterns and areas of solid color to play tricks with traditional perspective and depictions of space. In *Madame Vuillard Sewing* (fig. 16), an oil painting from the mid-1890s, Mme. Vuillard sits in the position typical of Vuillard's seamstresses: head bent, shoulders hunched, and hands close to the face.[18] Vuillard carefully positioned his mother as an island of monochromes in a sea of colored pattern. The middle part in her hair is centered

32

along the edge of the door frame, and her broad form extends across the door to the blue patterned wall, the dominant background of the composition. Almost matching the wall in size, the bulky duvet Mme. Vuillard is sewing stretches across the lower right half of the composition, its horizontal expanse emphasized by the red stripes that follow its form. The left third of the composition consists entirely of broadly painted monochromatic forms: the off-white of the door, which is defined by loose outlines, Mme. Vuillard with her white shirt and brown skirt, and a bright blue shape above an orange lozenge forming a flat strip along the left edge of the canvas. In the small oval painting of Mme. Vuillard (see fig. 10), the flatness of the composition was relieved by the placement of a foreshortened chair at lower left. Here the diagonal of the duvet's fold in the lower right corner indicates recession into a perspectival depth.

The stylistic differences in these works are minimal; Vuillard's paintings of single women sewing usually center around the isolated figure hunched over her work and surrounded by a heavily patterned, decorative, and ambiguous pictorial space. Vuillard used pattern to flatten the space but at the same time included a few subtle indications of traditional perspective, causing the composition to hover between a decorative surface and an illusion of three-dimensionality.

The hunched pose that Vuillard records in such paintings as *Seamstress (Interior)* (fig. 15) and *A Seamstress* (fig. 17) has its origins in fact. Vuillard's position as an observant youth in his mother's atelier would have given him ample opportunity to see the harsh realities of what an outsider might have considered a relatively genteel "cottage industry." In fact, the corset trade required long hours of its workers, particularly the assistants, like Vuillard's sister Marie, who performed the menial tasks of assembling and finishing the corsets. A 1907 essay in a Socialist journal chronicled the life and labors of "Mme. G," a typical *corsetière*.[19] The article described the steps a corsetmaker's assistant performed:

> The corsets consigned to the worker are cut out and basted for assembly or even already stitched. They have undergone a first fitting and adjustments have been made or are indicated by pins.
>
> Returning to her home, the worker stitches the corset, if this has not already been done; she mounts it, she laces it, rounds it, smooths it, bastes and stitches the braid or ribbons into which she threads the whalebones. She fixes them, puts the busc and the stays in place, fans out the corset, hems it, places the pads if it needs them, and applies the decorations. Corsets are delivered without the hooks, which are put on at the proprietress's. Corsets are from time to time lined, and the lining is put in at the last moment.[20]

Although the making of a corset required these various steps, they were not always performed by one individual. "Mme. G"—whose life shows many striking parallels to that of Mme. Vuillard—split the tasks so that she and her two daughters all worked on each corset according to "her knowledge and aptitudes."[21]

The demand for corsets or dresses varied according to season—January was the

33

15 ✤

Seamstress (Interior)

1892–95

oil on panel, 9¼ x 13½ inches, Yale

University Art Gallery, New Haven,

Connecticut; bequest of Edith Malvina K.

Wetmore

slowest month, the summer had a higher demand due to the tourist trade, and November was the busiest month for Parisian customers—and even a small workshop might be expected to produce an average of nine corsets per week. To accomplish this, an atelier sometimes had to operate thirteen or fourteen hours per day, including Sundays and holidays.[22] When the working hours are totaled, assuming an average working day of ten hours, "Mme. G" devoted a staggering 369 working days a year to the making of corsets! These long hours were possible because "Mme. G," like Vuillard's mother, worked at home; such a schedule would not have been permitted in a factory. Statistics reveal, in fact, that those who worked in a private home worked the longest hours and received the lowest wages.[23]

It was not Vuillard's intention, however, merely to record the specific details of his mother's workroom nor to chronicle the working conditions there for the purposes of sociological study. In fact, these paintings of women sewing constitute a visual demonstration of Stéphane Mallarmé's notion that one must express the effect something produces rather than the thing itself: "To name an object is to suppress three-fourths of the enjoyment . . . to suggest it, that is the dream."[24] These are portraits not of individuals, but of workers. Even if the sitter is identifiable, it is more by her pose or her gesture than by her physiognomy. Vuillard thus focused not on the features or even the psyche of his subject but rather on the figure's absorption into her environment, using color and form as metaphors for that relationship. In the Symbolist portrait Vuillard sought to evoke not the sitter specifically, but the world of work

16 ✤

Madame Vuillard Sewing

c. 1895

oil on panel, 7½ x 9⅜ inches, William

Kelly Simpson

34

in which she was immersed. Although he blurred the individuality of his subjects in these works, Vuillard always rooted his Symbolist sensibility in the familiar:

> Why is it in familiar places that one's spirit and sensibility find the most that is really novel? Novelty is always necessary to life, to consciousness.[25]

Vuillard spoke of finding a new spirit and sensibility in things and places that are familiar. Perhaps this accounts for his choosing to paint the subject closest to him again and again, constantly learning new things from familiar forms.

Vuillard's paintings of seamstresses, in familiar environments and performing familiar tasks, also depict an aspect of modern life. The hunched poses Vuillard recorded and the awkward points of view that he adopted might have been inspired

by passages in Edmond Duranty's often-quoted apologia of Naturalism, *La nouvelle peinture,* published in 1876:

> What we need are the special characteristics of the modern individual—in his clothing, in social situations, at home, or on the street . . . This is . . . the study of states of mind reflected by physiognomy and clothing. It is the study of the relationship of a man to his home, or the particular influence of his profession on him, as reflected in the gestures he makes: the observation of all aspects of the environment in which he evolves and develops.
>
> A back should reveal temperament, and social position, a pair of hands should reveal the magistrate or the merchant, and a gesture should reveal an entire range of feelings.[26]

The composition of Vuillard's paintings of women sewing became more complicated as the number of figures increased. Some of the early seamstress paintings, from 1891–92, are particularly refined in their compositional balance. *The Dressmakers* of 1891 (fig. 8), like the oval *Woman Mending* (see fig. 10), depends relatively little on the effects of pattern. Here flattened, monochrome forms are closely interlocked, showing the stylistic influence of Gauguin's and Sérusier's flat, sinuously contoured planes.[27] Vuillard adopted a dynamic point of view in this picture to offset the simplicity and flatness of the unmodulated shapes. The viewpoint in the paintings discussed thus far has been straightforward, and the composition fairly parallel to the picture plane. But here the artist loomed above the head of the foreground figure and then changed the point of view slightly to observe the figure in the background from a less dramatic angle. Although the forms appear parallel to the picture plane because of their lack of modeling, their extreme foreshortening modifies their contours and creates a strong sense of recession, thus establishing a tension between surface and depth. Vuillard's shapes, their edges receding into depth, take on a life of their own, giving to the composition as a whole a lyrical harmony. The painter alleviates any possibility of visual heaviness or monotony by leaving a thin outline of untouched canvas around each shape—a "halo" of tone that enlivens the pattern of the composition and enhances the work's subtle spatial paradox.

The sinuous curves of the composition, not unlike the works that Gauguin was painting concurrently in Tahiti, might be considered an early manifestation of the whiplash curves of art nouveau, the decorative offshoot of Symbolism, which dominated advanced aesthetic taste at the turn of the century. Expressing a keen sensibility for the design of a painting, Vuillard once mentioned how a composition could develop from a line or a shape:

> [to] express what I feel (it's a simple designation, an *act* pure and simple to designate the thing that I have in my head): an expression of tenderness caused by a certain object . . . Then I trace on the paper—in one blow, as they say, pure when an idea presents itself, the line or the imagined and wished-for shape . . . I develop it if need be and I compose, a simple deed in itself to compose and all my patience . . . is absorbed by the desire to do well, and thus the possibility of really prolonged manual work.[28]

A Seamstress

1892–93

oil on canvas, 25⅜ x 21 inches,

The Saint Louis Art Museum; gift of

Sydney M. Schoenberg, Sr.

In spite of evidence that he sometimes worked from a model—to paint such works as *Seated Nude* (fig. 19), for example[29]—Vuillard wanted to rely on his intellect, "to designate the thing that I have in my head," and to develop the composition around a remembered motif from nature, transformed by the imagination. He strove to produce the "imagined and wished-for shape."

In *The Dressmakers* the composition revolves around a central vortex. The curve of the rear figure's arm leads from the left side of the canvas to her head, then flows to the foreground figure's head and her arm, which completes the circle at the bottom right of the canvas. The sinuous shapes of the fabric enhance the flatness of the

37

composition. Color, too, plays an important role here, for as in the tiny painting of *Workers at the Chiffonnier* (fig. 18), Vuillard used strong, rich patches of unmodulated color to describe a flat and decorative surface.

Several ambiguously receding forms serve to complicate the pictorial space, so that it hovers between flatness and depth. For example, the seamstress in the foreground, most likely Mme. Vuillard, is cutting a piece of material. She holds a pair of scissors in her right hand, partially hidden beneath the fabric, and pulls away the cloth she has cut with her left. The space created between the two pieces reveals the table top with a spool of thread and the side of the table, which is painted dark brown. The red material, however, makes it almost impossible to recognize the beige and brown shapes as a table, in the same way that a figure sometimes placed by Vuillard at the corner of a wall prevents a clear perception of recession into depth.

This subjective deformation has its inspiration in Vuillard's desire to make his painting emotionally expressive. In September 1890 Vuillard wrote that the emotional response he had to a subject was more important than its physiognomy:

> A woman's head just gave to me a certain emotion; the emotion alone must be enough for me and I mustn't struggle to remember her nose or her ear, all that doesn't matter in the least.[30]

It is certain, too, that Vuillard's subjective manipulation of the objects he represented was motivated in part by his experience with Symbolist theory. Although Symbolism as a literary theory had been addressed as early as 1886, it was Albert Aurier who first fully set out a Symbolist doctrine for the visual arts in his article "Le Symbolisme en peinture: Paul Gauguin," published in the *Mercure de France* in March 1891. In this article Aurier outlined the characteristics of a Symbolist painting, concluding that:

> The strict duty of the ideological painter is to make a rational selection among the multiple elements combined in objectivity, to utilize in his work only the general and distinctive lines, forms, colors which serve to put down clearly the ideological significance of the object, in addition to some partial symbols which corroborate the general symbol. The artist will always have the right . . . to exaggerate, to attenuate, to deform these directly significant characters (forms, lines, colors, etc.) not only according to his individual vision, not only according to the form of his personal subjectivity (such as happens even with realistic art), but also to exaggerate, attenuate and deform them according to the needs of the idea to be expressed.[31]

Vuillard responded in his journal to two aspects of Aurier's essay: first, to the idea and emotional potency of the "symbol"—how the partial symbol relates to the whole—and second, to the more concrete aspects of the effect of the selective inclusion and deformation of forms:

> An admirable thing, the spirit which should in our case be the strongest, becomes the slave of the senses: one wants to *feel* or rather one only considers the emotions, and when it comes to reflecting, generalizing, symbolizing, one is powerless; one believes in the existence of a special or partial symbol; but it is only a symbol in relation to our spiritual operations! One needs as an absolute necessity for living . . . one needs a rhythmic whole, solid in conviction, in faith, a sort of key that would permit us to understand the signs.[32]

While other Symbolist painters looked to exotic or otherworldly subject matter for their pictures, Vuillard sought deeper meaning in subjects close at hand. In his self-portraits Vuillard gradually departed from his specific physiognomy to achieve a conjunction of method and meaning. This tactic is even more evident in his paintings of seamstresses, where the particular characteristics of individuals are always sacrificed to the greater harmony of the picture. The colors, lines, and patterns that Vuillard used to describe these women stand not only for the decorative nature of the product they were making but also for the harmony of the work of art, Vuillard's creation.

The Flowered Dress (La Robe à ramages) (fig. 20) from 1891 combines the flat forms of *The Dressmakers* with a layered patterning similar to the paintings of single *corsetières*. The resulting complexity of pictorial space and the rigorous compositional structure equal the best of Vuillard's mature work. Here three-dimensional spatial effects are particularly sophisticated, refuting the argument made by some scholars that in 1891, when this picture was painted, Vuillard was interested only in compositions parallel to the picture plane.[33] The background of the painting has been

Workers at the Chiffonnier

1892

oil on cardboard, 9¹/₁₆ x 12 inches,

Josefowitz Collection

Seated Nude

1892

oil on cardboard, 11½ x 8⅝ inches,

Josefowitz Collection

reduced to a pattern of vertical rectangles set off by the strong, light-colored horizontal of the mantelpiece above the middle figure. Although changes in background color suggest that the back wall is not flat, Vuillard deliberately left out any indication of corners by masking areas where the wall meets the floor or the ceiling and by painting the elements that are attached to the wall, such as the mantelpiece or the mirror above it, from a frontal point of view.

Each of the three figures is isolated against a different background element, but the actual placement of each in the room is difficult to decipher. The woman in the patterned dress on the right stretches to almost the full height of the composition, dwarfing the two figures to her left. Although the viewer normally would interpret her height as evidence that she stands in the extreme foreground of the composition,

20 ❧

The Flowered Dress

(La Robe à ramages)

1891

oil on canvas, 15 x 18⅛ inches, Museu de

Arte de São Paolo, Brazil

Vuillard introduced an element of spatial ambiguity by painting the left arm of the seamstress in the middle of the picture so that it overlaps the flowered dress of the larger woman to the right. This indicates—against all conventional rules of perspective—that the small, hunched over figure in the middle of the composition is in the foreground. The visual power of this small central figure is enhanced by the exaggerated breadth of her armspan in the composition: her elbows extend across almost half of the picture. By cutting the composition at the knees of the standing figure, Vuillard prevented the viewer from seeing where her feet are located on the floor and thus avoided indicating her precise location in the room. This ambiguity is increased because the standing figure wears a flowered dress and so dominates the rest of the picture, which is composed entirely of flatly colored shapes.

The composition is essentially divided into two parts, the right side consisting of large-scale forms, and the left of small forms, each separated by the vertical strip of wall to the right of the mantel. Yet the differences in scale between the right and the left sides of the composition do not encourage the viewer to read the composition as deep space. Rather, Vuillard created a series of surface balances: the visual weight of the figure in the flowered dress on the right matched by the two figures to the left. A small reflection of the figure's flowered dress, her neck, and her hair in the overmantel mirror establishes a sinuous curve that leads the eye from that reflection, to the monochromatic figure on the extreme left, to the central hunched over figure made of solid planes of color, and back to the large figure in the flowered dress. Vuillard painted a simple background to balance the right part of the composition, where the patterned dress is more forceful than the solid tones of the other women's garments. To balance the torsos on the left, he introduced a similar area of dark flat color on the right in the form of a black chair, which he reduced to a dark rectangle. The middle area plays the part of a compositional, visual, and perhaps even psychological caesura. The two sections of the painting denote two different spaces and activities.

As befits her dominant placement in the composition, the woman in the flowered dress is not sewing but instead gathering a large piece of material that may have been worked on already. Given the similarity of the dress to those worn by Marie Vuillard in other pictures, this figure may be Marie. Likewise, the huddled figure on the extreme left bears some resemblance to Vuillard's grandmother, Mme. Michaud, who is depicted in the corners of several compositions wearing the same dark headdress.[34]

A painting of a pair of women sewing reveals that Vuillard wove pattern, color, light, and perspective in many different ways. In *Beneath the Lamp* (fig. 21), dated 1892, two women sit at a table on either side of a lamp with a round green base and a dark shade. The figures in the painting, represented as black-garbed silhouettes, are depicted in flat colors.

While *The Flowered Dress* is characterized by a sophisticated balance between two kinds of surfaces, right and left coming forward and receding in turn, *Beneath the Lamp* is dominated by a succession of planes that heighten the tension between spatiality and flatness. At the top of the painting a strip of shadow runs in an even band across all the elements of the vertically divided back wall. Although the background comprises many elements—a red and black patterned wallpaper, a door jamb, two dark vertical stripes, and a window—Vuillard made it look flat by indicating the bottom of the wall only at the left, where the surface is parallel to the picture plane, thus encouraging the eye to read the rest of the back wall as a continuous surface. Yet below the table—the horizontal black and red strip in the middle of the canvas—a triangular shape indicates that the vertical stripes along the back wall actually constitute a screen that folds in and out.[35] The ambiguity of the screen's placement is further complicated by the direct visual link Vuillard created between the thin black line on the back wall and the lamp on the table, which continues its exact line into the middle ground of the canvas. Ursula Perucchi-Petri has noted Vuillard's roving point of view in this scene, where the armchair or sofa looming in the right foreground is depicted as if seen from above and the figures of women are observed at eye level.[36]

The figures themselves are defined by the arabesques of their flat silhouettes; Vuillard did not use highlight or shade to give them volume.[37] The severity of the silhouettes is offset by the colorful decorative accents that constitute the back wall. The figure at the left, who sits on a chair depicted in perspective, appears to be both sitting down with her full weight and floating like a two-dimensional paper cut-out. The curving outline of the chair at the right serves as a sinuous complement to her silhouette—reduced as it is from functional object to flat shape.

This duality of function is at the heart of Vuillard's aesthetic here. His use of shapes that are simultaneously recognizable objects and purely decorative forms awakens the viewer's eye to the complex layering of planes in the composition and encourages the viewer to read these planes in depth. On the other hand, Vuillard's use of varied patterns, painted with discernable thickness and dispersed evenly across the composition, encourages the viewer to read the painting as a "flat surface covered with colors in a certain order."

Beneath the Lamp is a tighter and more complex composition than other paintings of its type, with a more varied tonal range. *The Green Lamp* (fig. 22), which dates from 1892, is similar in composition and also has a limited palette of browns, beiges, and greens. Here three figures, seen in dark silhouette, hover around a table illuminated by the same green lamp that is the central element in the other pictures. In this painting, however, Vuillard seemed to concentrate on the dramatic shadow cast by the lamp on the background wall; the two connected lozenge shapes dominate the composition.

The room in which these women work appears shrouded in shadow and mystery, separate from any specific environment. This feeling of mystery is due, in part, to the dramatic shadows that make the room and its furnishings impenetrable and ominous. Comparison with other pictures painted at approximately the same time, however, sheds light on these mysterious elements. Certain clues in *The Green Lamp* indicate that it depicts the same room that is shown in daylight in *Interior with Women Sewing*

Beneath the Lamp

1892

oil on canvas, 12½ x 15¾ inches, Musée

de l'Annonciade, Saint-Tropez

(*L'Aiguillée*) (fig. 24) of 1893. The thin strip of pattern at the far side of the window—which must represent a panel of wallpaper—and the diagonal shape that cuts off the top of the window—which represents an elaborately framed portrait—are difficult to interpret in *The Green Lamp* but clearly indicated in *L'Aiguillée*.

As Vuillard backed up to reveal more of the surroundings in which his seam-stresses worked, his compositions increased in spatial complexity. Just as in *Beneath the Lamp* Vuillard introduced into the right foreground a large piece of furniture tilted in perspective, so he continued to use the lower corners of his pictures for objects that share the viewer's space and the illusory picture space to which the rest of the composition must refer. This device reappears in *L'Aiguillée*. A table, covered with several different pieces of fabric, stands in the lower right corner of the canvas, while the lower left corner reveals the crest- and backrails of a chair that appears to face away from the figures sewing and toward the viewer. This scene of women sewing exploits the motifs of silhouette and changing scale seen in Vuillard's earlier work and introduces the element of natural light, which plays an important role in his work from this point on. There are three women in this composition: the central figure with her back to the viewer, another who faces the viewer, and a third at the left of the canvas whose arm and torso are barely visible. As in the other pictures of women sewing, their features are obscured and their gestures are left to speak for them. The painting revolves around the silhouette of one of the women sewing but, unlike previous pictures where silhouettes are made by harsh artificial light or by flattened black clothing and the absence of modeling, her form loses three-dimensional definition because of the light streaming through the window beyond her.[38]

The origins of Vuillard's use of pure silhouettes are unclear; many artistic sources can be proposed. Perucchi-Petri attributes Vuillard's use of the silhouette to the influence of Japanese prints and points out that the silhouette had already been used by Manet, Degas, and Vallotton (although Vallotton and Vuillard surely were producing flat forms at much the same time).[39] She adds that Henri de Toulouse-Lautrec used the silhouette to great effect in posters, but in fact the poster designer Jules Chéret may have been as great an influence. Vuillard mentioned both his friend Lautrec and Chéret in his journal:

> It's an astonishing thing [to see] a Chéret beside a Lautrec. Just because a design is more or less black and just because its lines are more or less bold is no reason that it should be more or less significant.[40]

Retrospectives of Georges Seurat's work at the Salon des Indépendants in the spring of 1892 and again at the offices of the *Revue Blanche* at the end of that year would have

44

given Vuillard an opportunity to see once more such works as *La Parade* (1887–88, The Metropolitan Museum of Art), in which silhouettes are exploited to great effect. While Seurat's scientific, reductive approach to painting is different from Vuillard's, the depiction of iconic figures in stiff, sometimes hieratic postures is common to both.

Vuillard also would have seen the works of Utamaro and Hiroshige at an exhibition at the Galerie Durand-Ruel in January 1893, the year he completed *L'Aiguillée.* Vuillard's fascination with things Japanese can be traced back to early 1888, when he wrote the words "dessins japonais" in his journal without further elaboration.[41] Pages 12v–25 in the journal's second volume are full of ink drawings in the Japanese style, with articulated outlines and dramatic sweeps of the brush (figs. 25 and 26). Page 13 actually depicts an Oriental woman, and the edges of subsequent pages are decorated with drawings that resemble calligraphy. Because they precede the first journal entry, which is dated September 1890, these drawings must date from that year and indicate an interest in Japanese art several years before *L'Aiguillée*.[42] Japanese prints might have influenced Vuillard both in their style, which stressed the dynamic power of curving lines, the compounding of several points of view in the same work, and the decorative appeal of sinuous shapes in flat colors, and to a lesser but important degree in their subject matter, which was often devoted to scenes of women in the home.

Thadée Natanson, one of Vuillard's greatest patrons and a close friend, in his review of the 1893 exhibition at Galerie Durand-Ruel for *La Revue Blanche,* discussed the subjects of the prints in terms that recall Vuillard's own writing about the decorative quality of these works. Most of these prints, Natanson wrote, "have only a very simple subject or no subject at all, for it has been enough to represent a woman's pose, that of two women side by side, or that of a mother and a baby. . . . A line has been enough to indicate the outline of the nose, the arch of the eyes . . . the modeling or the color of the flesh. Utamaro has pushed further the search for ornamental and decorative value of lines and colors, patiently establishing the significance of forms."

In his reaction to Japanese imagery, Natanson, like Vuillard, revealed an aesthetic sensibility attuned to the niceties of pictorial composition. In Utamaro's work, it was the "arrangement of the composition that charms"; the great Japanese artist, Natanson believed, "was preoccupied . . . by the ornamental and decorative value of forms, loves these and clings to them for themselves, for their pictorial significance and their design." He argued, finally, that the artist "studied forms in minute detail with love and patience, only so he could express their decorative significance."[43]

Just as Vuillard wanted to create a painting based on the emotional impression he received from a moment of conjunction with his subject, in order to create a

25

Sketches from Vuillard's journal, 1890,

EV I.2, 12v–13, Bibliothèque de l'Institut

de France, Paris

26

Sketches from Vuillard's journal, 1890,

EV I.2, 19v–20, Bibliothèque de l'Institut

de France, Paris

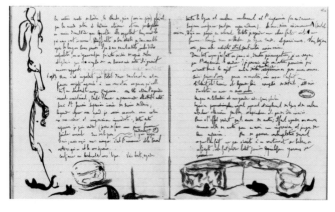

46

comprehensive, "decorative" work of art, so the Japanese artist, in Thadée Natanson's analysis, best succeeded when he surrendered the detail to the effect of the whole. Natanson attributes the power of Utamaro's work to his ability to concentrate on the independent ornamental and decorative aspects of his subjects, eschewing naturalistic depiction. Vuillard had said much the same thing when he vowed to dispense with recording details—the nose or the ear—that meant nothing to the work as a whole.

Thus the emotional power of the central figure in *L'Aiguillée* depends not on any individual feature but upon her silhouette, which constitutes her "ornamental and decorative value." This is emphasized not only because of the strength of her monochrome black form but also because her outline spans the entire center of the painting. Her gesture is made iconic by its isolation against the window, creating a simple, stark, dark-on-light contrast to which the viewer's gaze constantly returns.

Although Vuillard has painted a window here, the painting's colors are not reduced to a blinding whiteness, as they would be in direct light, nor is there a uniform distribution of light and shadow. Because he painted the objects on the foreground table with such clarity of color and brightness, Vuillard encouraged the viewer to assume the existence of a second source of light.[44] In the same way that he created an arbitrary horizontal division of light in *Beneath the Lamp,* here Vuillard divides light and shadow horizontally in the background: light streaming through the window creates a rectangle of sunshine on the back wall, highlights obliterate the features of the rear woman's face, and the objects in front of her on the table remain in shadow. Similarly, in a painting of *Madame Vuillard at Her Desk* (fig. 29), sunlight creates an arbitrary "panel" against a paneled door, part of a series of rectilinear forms that set off the silhouette of Mme. Vuillard, her chair, her desk, and the lamp; and in *Madame Roussel at the Chiffonnier* (fig. 30), the bulk of the dresser partially obscures the source of light, a window at the far right, shown as a bright rectangle in the upper corner of the painting.

The Seamstress in the Indianapolis Museum of Art (fig. 31) was painted in the same year as *L'Aiguillée* and depicts the same arrangement of furniture. It shows a woman sewing in front of the same window but from farther away. The thin patterned strip of wall beyond the window in *L'Aiguillée* is also present in this picture, but another strip of the same wallpaper in the extreme left foreground indicates that we might be seeing this woman from the vantage point of another room. The back wall, which is a solid color in *L'Aiguillée,* is shown here with yet another pattern of wallpaper, similar to the one seen in *The Seamstress* of 1891 (see fig. 11).

The figure in the Indianapolis painting is posed much like the right-hand figure in *Dressmakers Under the Lamp* (see fig. 23), indicating that Vuillard often reused a pose and did not necessarily compose each scene from life. As his journal from 1888 indicates, Vuillard made sketches of subjects years before he actually painted them. Indeed, he wrote in 1890 that he had sufficient material in his journals to paint from for many years to come:

27 ❦

Interior (Interior at l'Etang-la-Ville)

1893

oil on canvas, 13 x 16 inches, from the

Private Collection of Jane Forbes Clark

> Delve into the idea that I already have enough to occupy myself for years in developing
> and using and making into art all the things I have in my notebooks and boxes.[45]

These images served almost as a stock from which Vuillard could select at will,
enabling him to separate himself from the actual scene at hand and to create instead
compositions that conveyed his ideas.

28 ❦

Interior (L'Atelier)

1893

oil on millboard panel, 12½ x 14¹⁵⁄₁₆

inches, Smith College Museum of Art,

Northampton, Massachusetts; purchased

1938

Perhaps the most complex of Vuillard's sewing pictures is *Interior (L'Atelier)* (fig. 28),
painted in the same year as *L'Aiguillée* (see fig. 24). It combines the layering of
patterns usually seen in paintings of single women sewing with the decorative use of
silhouette common to paintings of groups of women at work. The spatial complexities
of this picture are as sophisticated as any in Vuillard's oeuvre: the deliberate confusion
of planes makes the background appear to come forward as a flat surface parallel to the
picture plane, while at the same time visual cues indicate a floor that recedes into
depth.

    The three figures in this composition serve as stable points around which the
decorative objects in the room swirl. In contrast to *Madame Roussel at the Chiffonnier*
(see fig. 30), or even to *L'Aiguillée,* the background here shows a subtle variation of

pattern, one blending into another. The cupboard on the left, with its top and its bottom painted at perspectival angles, functions as a visual point of stasis in the composition because of its specific location in space and its strong, flat orange color. This solid orange finds its complement in the length of blue fabric that stretches across almost the entire width of the composition, encouraging the viewer's eye to span the painting.

Although Vuillard may have intended this blue cloth to function as a divider between the simple foreground and the highly patterned background of the painting, he complicated a clear reading of the space by clothing the figure in the left

49

29 ❧

Madame Vuillard at Her

Desk

1892

oil on canvas, 16⅜ x 13 inches, Galerie

Jan Krugier: Geneva

30 ❧

Madame Roussel at the

Chiffonnier

c. 1894

oil on composition board, 11½ x 8½

inches, Eastlake Gallery Inc., New York

foreground of the painting in a densely spotted dress that merges with the flowered pattern of the wallpaper beyond. The young woman, probably Marie Vuillard, literally blends into the *ground* of the painting since her spotted dress is composed of a network of black dots scattered over the blank, unpainted surface of the cardboard. Although the skirt of her dress extends to the bottom of the canvas, her feet are not shown, leaving her exact position unclear. Marie's head blends with the wallpaper as much as her torso does. Her hair is indicated by a few brown accents, allowing the cardboard again to be an active element, this time as a highlight. Although she is seen from behind, her face, painted in two tones of gray, turns toward the light emanating from the window at the right of the composition.

A man, clothed in a dark solid jacket, enters the room through a door covered in the same paper as the wall.[46] The door is differentiated from the wall by a subtle darkness in tone: opening away from the window, it would be cast in shadow. Vuillard also indicated that part of the back wall lies behind the glass of the open window. A smudge in the top pane of glass shows that light is hitting it, and the wallpaper behind it is slightly grayer in tone.

When Vuillard painted the window itself, the source of light for the picture, he added to the profusion of pattern in the picture by painting a rectangle of white, yellow, and peach dots as opaque as the wallpaper. A few small splashes of brown suggest that the white dots might be blossoms on the branches of a tree, but the tree would have been only the departure point for Vuillard's patterning. At the left side of the window, a patterning of these light dots in between darker lines suggests the grid of a lattice.

31 ❧

The Seamstress

1893

oil on composition board, 11½ x 10¼

inches, © Indianapolis Museum of Art;

anonymous gift in memory of Caroline

Marmon Fesler

32

The Window

c. 1893

oil on canvas, 14¾ x 18 inches,

Collection: William S. Paley, New York

The transition from foreground to middle ground in the composition has been deliberately confused. As in *L'Aiguillée* a tabletop in the right foreground is bisected, leaving no clear indication of its actual orientation; it appears to tip to face the viewer.[47] The jumble of material on this table visually leads to the scattered material on the table in the middle of the composition. This latter table is of the drop-leaf type, as the extended gate leg is visible on the left of the picture. But the way the table stretches across almost the entire composition is not entirely logical, since it recedes diagonally on the left while remaining parallel to the picture plane on the right.

The painting's subject, like its form, resists easy interpretation. The confrontation between the young woman and the bearded man in *L'Atelier* often has been seen as a subtle reference to the impending marriage of Vuillard's sister to Ker-Xavier Roussel, and this hypothesis might explain the feeling the painting gives of containing a secret message.[48] Certainly the introduction of a man into these almost exclusively female sewing pictures is an oddity in Vuillard's work, for although men often are included in his pictures of the family dining and in his series of paintings of Misia Natanson (see "The Drama of Daily Life" and "The Music of Painting"), except for this example Vuillard's sewing paintings are exclusively devoted to women. Nevertheless, although he occupies the center of the composition, Roussel is half hidden by the door, indicating that he is no more than an intruder in this world of women.

Vuillard's consistent choice of women as the subject matter for his work was deliberate, and he wrote about it at length a short while after he painted this picture:

> In the aspects that I choose when so to speak I observe, to draw out subjects for painting or for contemplating painting I realize that up till now I have only barely assembled, composed if you will, rather informed *attempts*, despite the belief, which is nothing but a trickery and a lack of reflection on my part, that I am indifferent to objects presented to my eyes, I ought to have had a varied multitude of objects represented in my paintings, but I never put male persons into them, I realize. On the other hand, when my purpose tends to men, I always see burdened wretches, I have only the feeling of ridiculous objects. Never [so] in front of women, where I always find a way to isolate a few elements that satisfy the painter in me. But the ones are not uglier than the others. They only are in my imagination.[49]

Curiously, for all the frankness with which he states his preference for woman as subject matter, he does not address his own role in the woman's world that he paints. It is tempting to surmise that Vuillard felt himself to be an intruder, perhaps even a voyeur—as he had characterized his friend Roussel in *L'Atelier*.

A space very similar to that in *L'Atelier* is the subject of another picture, *Interior* (fig. 27). The painting has sometimes been called *Interior at l'Etang-la-Ville*, but since it is dated 1893, the interior must be that of that painter's apartment on the rue St. Honoré and not that of his sister's house at l'Etang-la-Ville, where Marie and Roussel moved only late in the decade. In *Interior*, Vuillard could not resist the inclusion of one spatial anomaly—a tiny chair, seen from above and covered with material. The eye has to shift from the chair, depicted from one point of view, to the foreground table, painted on a different scale and from another angle. The gate-leg table from *L'Atelier* is also here in the background, as is the lattice work in the windows.

The Window (fig. 32), another painting in this series of works devoted to the atelier, offers a view of three walls of a room; this stage-set perspective enables the viewer to recognize elements of the room in other paintings. A woman, probably Marie Vuillard, stands in front of a chest of drawers, beside a full-length French door.[50] At the left a wall recedes into the background, interrupted by a door that is covered, like the one in *L'Atelier,* in wallpaper. On the right side of the canvas, however, Vuillard has shown a door with a glass panel and a transom at the end of a wall of glass clerestory windows. These are the same windows visible in the lithograph *La Couturière* (see fig. 13), as well as the distinctive feature in the Phillips Collection's *Interior* (fig. 33).[51]

The table in the right foreground in *Woman by the Window* may be the same one seen in so many other pictures; beside it, overlapping the rectangle of the window, is an old-fashioned side chair like the one seen in the foreground of *L'Aiguillée.* The bustle of activity that distinguishes *L'Aiguillée,* on the other hand, is absent in this contemplative painting. Some action is implied, however, in Marie's pose: her torso faces the room and her head is turned back as if in response to something occurring outside the picture.

We shall see later that this room was also used by the Vuillard family as a dining room. Of interest at this point, and of potential relevance to the subject matter of Vuillard's paintings, is the fact that the family of "Mme. G," the *corsetière de Raincy,* also used the dining room as a workroom. They ate in the dining room only on Sundays, for on the other days they took their meals in the kitchen because the "service was quicker and the work could be left in the dining room."[52]

A description of the *corsetière's* house mentions that there were four principal rooms: two bedrooms, a dining room, and a kitchen. In addition, a *cabinet de toilette* served as both cloakroom and linen room.[53] Vuillard's apartments contained no more than two bedrooms but always seemed to have a salon in addition to a dining room.[54] Of course the various proportions of the apartments could have been quite different; certainly the Vuillards led a more bourgeois life than did "Mme. G." The difference in social rank would have been that of *patronne* to worker, the former living in the center of Paris, the latter in the suburbs.

But even if the erstwhile dining room was the center of activity for Mme. Vuillard's workers, sewing must have been going on all over the house. Vuillard's *Three Women in a Room with Rose-colored Wallpaper* (fig. 34) is closely related both in theme and in composition to a series of decorations he painted for the Desmarais family.[55] Here workers carry and arrange fabrics and clothing in what appears to be a bedroom, judging from the mid-nineteenth-century bed against the wall at the right. *The Atelier* (see frontispiece), a study for one of the Desmarais decorations, presents

53

33 ❧

Interior

1894

oil on cardboard mounted on canvas, 10¼

x 20 inches, The Phillips Collection,

Washington, D.C.

34 ❧

Three Women in a Room

with Rose-colored Wallpaper

1895

oil on cardboard, 12¾ x 20¾ inches,

Josefowitz Collection

even more workers arranged as if in a Japanese screen against a background of tables and chairs, walls and doors. One wonders if there were any room in the crowded apartment to which Vuillard could retreat to be alone, or if there were seamstresses in every corner of the world in which he lived.

It is only upon careful examination of many works on the same theme that one begins to understand Vuillard's pictorial vocabulary, the very private language that Vuillard shared so intimately with the people and the places closest to him. Each picture gives a clue to another, permitting his world to reveal itself step by step.

Perhaps the most perplexing aspect of these paintings is that they do not appear to record the principal activity of Mme. Vuillard's atelier—the making of corsets. Although it is certain that Vuillard's mother was a corsetmaker, not one of the paintings of women sewing depicts a corset being made. Generous lengths of fabric are most often seen, with the actual garments being sewn left undefined. The painter seldom included references to sewing machines, although they were commonly used at this time, and when he did depict machines, it was only in fragmentary glimpses.[56] Because Vuillard used the same figures in different compositions over a period of several years, sometimes even referring to fairly early sketches in his journal, these scenes clearly come as much from imagination as from reality.

The paintings of women sewing stand out in Vuillard's oeuvre for their decorative beauty, their complex construction, and their sense of intimacy. The figures in the compositions are depicted either alone or as isolated members of a group, and their features are never described. Even the pictures of pairs or groups of women give no sense of active communication between the figures: only the silent camaraderie of working women, each performing a specific function toward the creation of a finished product.

The sewing paintings are icons of the inwardness that informed Vuillard's personal approach to Symbolism. Objects do not stand for specific otherworldly concepts in these paintings, but through tightly woven space dominated by busy patterns they evoke a feeling of intimacy. Pattern is the unifying visual characteristic of these compositions, as might befit a body of work that has as its subject the working of cloth; ironically, the material being sewn is rarely decoratively patterned itself but almost always a solid color. Similarly, figures themselves—as flat, dark, and solid silhouettes—become decorative motifs in the paintings. It is the ensemble of the composition rather than its parts that constitutes it as decorative, harmonious, and intimate, thus adhering to Aurier's specifications for a Symbolist painting and answering Mallarmé's cry for a work of art that evokes a mood and a mystery rather than merely naming reality. These pictures also serve as metaphors for Vuillard's concept of himself as a painter. In depicting women conjoined with their surroundings much like the patterns of the objects they sew, Vuillard in some way reflects the union between the artist and the work he creates.

55

THE DRAMA OF DAILY LIFE:

THE ARTIST'S FAMILY

Thus the idea of the life surrounding us, of our life, source of all our

thoughts and productions, this becomes modernism . . .

EV I.2, 51 (26 October 1894)

35 🪴

Mother and Sister of the

Artist

c. 1892

oil on panel, 14⅝ x 10½ inches,

private collection

Vuillard seemed to turn to different subjects not only to evoke a variety of moods but also to express quite different artistic purposes. In the sewing paintings he focused on the act of work, an act he imbued with a sense of sanctity. By blurring the features of his sitters, Vuillard subordinated the identity of the laborer to the labor itself and conferred upon their work a sense of beauty and repose through a tight interweaving of line and color, silhouette and pattern. In his paintings of the family in the interior, by contrast, Vuillard shifted his emphasis to the family members themselves—their personalities and their ambiguous and often troubled relations with one another. Nevertheless, these works as much as the sewing pictures constitute his personal response to Symbolism. The sense of intense privacy, almost of a secret language, that hangs over the Vuillard family addresses the Symbolist aesthetic as eloquently as the decorative language of the paintings of seamstresses.

Many of Vuillard's paintings of his family in their various apartments revolve around the theme of dining. Vuillard's mother and sister are often shown at the table eating breakfast or drinking coffee; other paintings show more conventional meals, with a number of figures engaged in conversation; still others record with uneasy irony the aftermath of these interactions—they become images of supplication, embarrassment, or hurt feelings.

This sense of psychological drama is present in the earliest of Vuillard's images of his family gathered at the table. Although some scholars have seen in *Family of the Artist (L'Heure du dîner)* (fig. 36), painted in 1889, evidence of Vuillard's sense of humor, the work seems full of grim portents. Vuillard's mother, featureless and bent over the dining table, dominates the picture, while the other figures—his grandmother, his sister and, peering anxiously from a doorway, the painter himself—seem relegated to the background by Mme. Vuillard's bulk. The grandmother is shrouded and almost supplicating, and Marie seems frozen in place. The stark pallor of the wall behind Mme. Vuillard is broken by a lamp at the left, a candle burning to the right, and a painting that looms ominously over the rough form of the grandmother. This painting's position on the wall is ambiguous: the strong diagonal of its left edge indicates a steep overhang, but its right edge, parallel to the door, suggests that it hangs flat.

The subject matter and dark tone of *Family of the Artist* reflect the work of the Dutch masters whom Vuillard had admired, but the claustrophobic and airless atmosphere that permeates the painting is Vuillard's own. Diners in Dutch paintings can be counted on to go at their meal with gusto, if not riotousness, while the figures in *Family of the Artist* neither eat nor drink. Speechless, they seem closed in upon themselves. Vuillard's Dutch inspiration is also evident in *The Landing, rue de Miromesnil,* painted in 1891 (fig. 37). The sense of dislocation, emphasized both by the viewer's ambiguous relationship to the staircase and the landing and by the shadowy figure's hovering stance in an unseen doorway, is a Symbolist transformation of the logically organized hallways in the interior scenes of both Jan Vermeer and Jan

36 ❧

Family of the Artist

(L'Heure du dîner)

c. 1889

oil on canvas, 28¼ x 36⅜ inches,

The Museum of Modern Art, New York;

gift of Mr. and Mrs. Sam Salz and an

anonymous donor

37 ❧

The Landing, rue de

Miromesnil

1891

oil on canvas, 15½ x 9¼ inches, Mrs.

Samuel Godfrey

Steen. The location of *Family of the Artist* was probably also the Vuillard apartment on the rue de Miromesnil; the shared sense of foreboding clearly unites these two paintings of the same place.

An Outspoken Dinner Party (Le Dîner vert) (fig. 38) presents a different mood. The painter's family again is seated at the table. Vuillard's grandmother, Mme. Michaud, is depicted in caricatural profile on the left, his sister Marie and his brother Alexandre occupy the center of the picture, and Mme. Vuillard is at the right. Although Jacques Salomon described this scene as painted "from life" and stated that "no changes were made in the arrangement of things as they appeared to him [Vuillard] as he rose from the table," Vuillard has depicted a scene edited for pictorial effect.[1]

In fact, sketches of scenes of the family dining appear in Vuillard's journal as far back as 1888 (fig. 39; see fig. 42). A preparatory sketch (fig. 40) shows a lamp hanging from the ceiling in the center of the composition, but in the painting Vuillard obliterated the outline of the object and left only a dark square. The square, which evokes the same sense of hovering mystery as the similarly abstracted black and red form in *The Seamstress* (see fig. 11), unifies the rest of the painting. The square's color and density tie it to the dark silhouette of Vuillard's grandmother and the two wine bottles on the table, which are depicted simply as flat black shapes. Vuillard completed the interplay of dark shapes by balancing his grandmother's somber dress on the left with his mother's skirt across the canvas.

Vuillard's sister Marie is the focus of the painting. Her unusual and animated pose,[2] the lively pattern of her dress, and the air of amused engagement with which her head rests on her hand draw the viewer's attention to her. Mme. Vuillard's pose makes it clear that Marie has caught her attention, too. These two figures reappear in *Mother and Sister of the Artist* (fig. 35) where Vuillard depicted Marie in a similar position at the table. In this painting Vuillard pays considerable attention to the boldly patterned dresses that Marie and Mme. Vuillard wear.

Alexandre, Vuillard's older brother, whom he nicknames "Miguen" in his journals, appears a bit remote from the rest of the family in *An Outspoken Dinner Party,* smoking his pipe and leaning back in his chair. The brightness of Alexandre's shirt, however, contrasted with the dark silhouette of the wine bottles, brings him forward to form an important visual link between the other figures. Although the actual source of light is not visible, all the figures are bathed in the yellow glow from the chandelier above them.

Rather than accepting the scene as it was "when he rose from the table," Vuillard played with perspectival effects by placing the heads of the three women on the same horizontal plane. Despite the fact that Marie sits behind the table, far from the picture plane, the bright pattern of her dress, in contrast to the flat colors of the other figures, makes her appear to come to the foreground of the picture. In Vuillard's sketch for this composition, although she is in the same position behind the table, she is evidently farther back in the picture space since the drawing shows more of the tabletop and less of Marie. Vuillard flattened this effect in the painting by compress-

38 ❧

An Outspoken Dinner Party

(Le Dîner vert)

c. 1891

oil on canvas, 13¼ x 19¾ inches,

private collection, London

39

Sketches from Vuillard's journal showing

women around the table, 1888, EV I.1,

11v–12, Bibliothèque de l'Institut de

France, Paris

40

Sketch for Le Dîner vert, c. 1891, china

ink on paper, Mrs. Charles Goldman,

New York

ing the elements on the table, such as bowls and wine bottles, and by enlarging the figure of his sister. In another spatial anomaly, we see the figures in the painting head on, but the table is tipped slightly so that the objects on it are visible. The altered perspective of the table is emphasized by the two round dishes that Vuillard painted, one above the other and without overlapping, from exactly the same perspective angle.

The silhouetted figure of Mme. Michaud is also psychologically removed from the scene because of her placement and the way she is painted. Although one assumes she sits at the table, her legs do not appear to go under the top of it but rather, because of the flatness of her silhouette, to be placed parallel to the picture plane with the table behind her. The very starkness of the contrast of unmodeled dark and light also separates her from the others.

An Outspoken Dinner Party is less than half the size of *Family of the Artist,* and the figures themselves are smaller relative to the whole composition. The overall effect of *An Outspoken Dinner Party,* therefore, is more intimate. The colors are brighter and more varied, and the figures are unified by a central light source. Vuillard has created in this painting a greater sense of psychological and physical connection between the family members.

The *Vuillard Family at Lunch* of about 1896 (fig. 41) is the most representative of Vuillard's depictions of his family dining, much in the same way that *L'Atelier* (see fig. 28) is a summation of Vuillard's sewing imagery. Here, as in *An Outspoken Dinner Party,* Vuillard's grandmother is depicted in profile on the left while his mother is seated at the right margin of the canvas. A servant is shown through an open door at the right. Miguen is missing from this scene, but Marie takes her regular place at the opposite side of the table. In this picture, however, her head is almost completely obscured by a lamp hanging from the ceiling.

The hanging lamp, so central to the composition in *The Vuillard Family at Lunch,* constitutes an important decorative element in many of Vuillard's paintings of his family at the table. In those sewing pictures where lamps play an important role (see figs. 21, 22, and 32), they function as a light source as well as a decorative motif, the lamplight becoming a visual focus of the canvas. It is Vuillard's placement of the lamps and his attenuation of light and shadow that make the lamplit sewing scenes so dynamic. In the dining paintings, on the other hand, the shape of the lamp itself rather than the light it casts is the focus of Vuillard's attention: lamps appear to be important to the composition as much for what they obscure as for what they illuminate.

Thus, the lamp in *Family of the Artist* is not the principal source of light for the composition since it highlights Mme. Vuillard's face but not her torso, leaves Vuillard's grandmother entirely in shadow, and casts capricious light on Marie and Vuillard. Instead, the back wall is bathed in light from a candle that remains almost invisible to the viewer. In *An Outspoken Dinner Party* the overhead lamp sheds a circular pattern of light that creates an embracing umbrella, yet Vuillard's grandmother once again is not lit in the same way as the other figures. Finally, in *The Vuillard Family at Lunch* the overhead lamp commands attention but sheds no light. In his journals Vuillard provided an oblique explanation for these phenomena in his observations of everyday objects around him:

> One lives surrounded by *decorated* objects. In the most ordinary interior, there's not an object the form of which doesn't have an ornamental pretension—and most of the time the form hides its function from us under these irrelevant embellishments.[3]

As the lamp hides its function beneath its ornament, so Vuillard turned the light source against itself, using it to mask rather than to illuminate. The lamp that casts no light, or inadequate light, is a striking image in the dining paintings—no less so

41

The Vuillard Family at

Lunch

c. 1896

oil on canvas, 12½ x 18 inches, private

collection, New York

42

Sketch from Vuillard's journal showing

figures around a table, 1888, EV I.1,

10v–11, Bibliothèque de l'Institut de

France, Paris

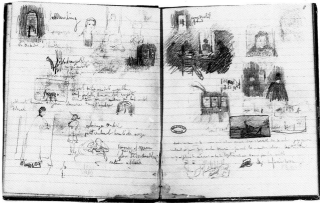

because Vuillard resorted to it so frequently. In the lithograph *Intérieur aux Teintures Roses II*, for example, from the series *Paysages et Intérieurs* that was published by Ambroise Vollard in 1899, a chandelier dominated the composition, blocking the head of a figure pushed to the extreme left corner of the page, as the lamp in *The Vuillard Family at Lunch* blocks Marie.[4] Even when the lamps are lit, Vuillard's characters remain incomplete and obscure, adding to the sense of a world apart, distant from the viewer.

The window is the source of light in *The Vuillard Family at Lunch* that illuminates Mme. Vuillard's face and hands and traces a path along the table toward the viewer. The light also reduces Vuillard's grandmother to a rather grotesque caricature by highlighting the extremities of her profile. Although we know by the indication of daylight that this is lunchtime, the painting has a dark, brooding mood.

The motif of placing figures in front of a window may have originated in a sketch in Vuillard's journal from 1888 (fig. 42). Vuillard conceivably spent years mulling over this composition with its characteristic air of psychological dislocation. The strange absence of interaction among the characters is emphasized by the bizarrely obscured silhouette of Marie, the central figure in the canvas, and by the enigmatic figure of a housekeeper at the right who seems almost to have stumbled onto the

43 ✣

Kitchen by Candlelight

1893

oil on canvas, 10⅝ x 8¼ inches, collection

of Aaron Fleischman, Washington, D.C.

64

scene. Her features are barely indicated and her torso is depicted as a flat black and olive arabesque.

The spatial qualities of *The Vuillard Family at Lunch,* or indeed any of the scenes of the family dining, set it apart from equivalent paintings of sewing themes. Typically, Vuillard based the composition of a painting devoted to sewing, such as *L'Atelier* (see fig. 28), on a tight structure of background elements that creates an impression of decorative flatness, offset by a few contradictory indications of depth. This painting of the Vuillard family dining is built on a structure that, although still relying on a mixture of patterns, is darker, denser, and more claustrophobic.

The background is a succession of vertical panels of equal width across the canvas, sometimes formed arbitrarily, as on the left where Vuillard introduced a vertical ray of light. The table that occupies the foreground space is tipped toward the viewer, although the perspective of objects on the table varies: the plate with a drumstick in the extreme foreground—perhaps at Vuillard's place—is depicted as if the viewer were standing directly above it, while the three carafes of wine farther back are seen head-on. The painter further confused the space by making the carafe of red wine appear to be behind and above the bottle of white wine or water in the foreground. It is as if Vuillard, standing uncomfortably close to the motif, made use of a shifting point of view—looking down at his own place setting and looking across the table at his sister.

A few details—the window that abuts a door and the white-framed panel of wall behind Mme. Vuillard—make it possible to conclude that the Vuillard family is dining in the room represented in such works as *The Window* (see fig. 32) and the lithograph *La Couturière* (see fig. 13), namely the dining room of the apartment at 346, rue St. Honoré. Again, from the varieties of activities that Vuillard sets in his pictures of this room, it is evident that the Vuillard family, like the *corsetière de Raincy,* worked and dined in the same space.[5]

The room connected to the kitchen by the door beside the large window and the series of interior windows seen from the other side appear in *Kitchen by Candlelight* (fig. 43), from about 1893. Here the unmodulated flat planes are a solemn contrast to the patterns of the dining room. Painted in somber greens, browns, and grays, this thinly worked monochrome study recalls the contemporary works of the Symbolist painter Eugène Carrière, both in its technique and its tenebrist, poetic mood.

Vuillard painted another picture of a kitchen during these same years: *The Kitchen (La Cuisine)* (fig. 44) is a condensed still life notable for the dot-patterned blue and white tile that lines part of the counter and the backsplash. The work's small scale and the pointillist application of paint indicate that it might have been painted as early as 1892 when Vuillard was experimenting briefly with a pointillist phase. But a corner of this tiled wall seems to be represented at the extreme left in *Woman at the Cupboard* of 1895 (fig. 45). Here a woman, perhaps Mme. Vuillard, is shown engaged in some chore, seen through an open door. The action takes up just over a third of the canvas; the right side is entirely composed of windows with wood frames and a

65

wainscot. The door, indicated by a handle, further confuses a clear reading of the space. Vuillard uses a similar compositional motif in *The Yellow Curtain* (fig. 46) where the action takes place in a small part of the canvas. Yet Vuillard condenses so much visual activity in this small section of the composition that the eye needs the repose offered by the dominant solid areas of calm color.

Vuillard and his mother moved to 346, rue St. Honoré in 1893.[6] In that year Vuillard's sister Marie married Roussel, so perhaps it was this shift in the makeup of the Vuillard family that occasioned the change in living arrangements for the painter and his mother. The move to the rue St. Honoré was probably not a wrenching one, for Mme. Vuillard and her son had inhabited this neighborhood for many years. Indeed, the commercial neighborhoods around the Opéra and the boulevards had been their home since 1877, when they moved to Paris from Vuillard's birthplace of Cuiseaux, a small town in the Jura. At first the family had lived with the Michauds, Mme. Vuillard's parents, in the rue de Chabrol near the Gare de l'Est. When Mme. Vuillard took over the corset-making business from Mme. Duval-Caron in about 1878–79, the Vuillard family moved to the rue Neuve St.-Augustin, later renamed the rue Daunou. This street connects the avenue de l'Opéra to the Boulevard des Capucines and thus was a more central location for a corsetmaker than the residence they had shared with Mme. Vuillard's parents since the entire clothing industry was concentrated in the area around the Opéra.

44 ❧

The Kitchen (La Cuisine)

1892

oil on composition board, 6¾ x 13¼

inches, Yale University Art Gallery, New

Haven, Connecticut; gift of James L.

Goodwin, B.A. 1905, Henry Sage

Goodwin, B.A. 1927, and Richmond L.

Brown, B.A. 1907

In 1884 M. Vuillard died. In the next year when the building at 20, rue Daunou was destroyed to make way for the Samaritaine de Luxe, the more luxurious branch of the well-known department store, Mme. Vuillard and her three children moved to 6, rue du Marché St. Honoré, which was only a few blocks away. At her new address Mme. Vuillard was listed as *Fab't de corset vendant en détail*—a retail manufacturer of corsets. From the Marché St. Honoré, the family moved to 10, rue de Miromesnil, where Vuillard painted *Family of the Artist* and *The Landing, rue de Miromesnil*. Although this location was just to the west of the Opéra district, the family moved back to the more central rue St. Honoré in 1893.

Vuillard and his mother lived at 346, rue St. Honoré for approximately four years. The family's next move, in 1897, was to the building almost next door; they

45 🌭

Woman at the Cupboard

1895

oil on paper mounted on wood, 14⅝ x

13⅛ inches, Wallraf-Richartz-Museum,

Cologne

stayed for only one year at 342, rue St. Honoré.[7] By 1898 Vuillard was an artist of some repute, having received no less than four commissions to paint decorative panels in various Parisian homes.[8] He could now support his mother with his earnings. In that year, when Mme. Vuillard was fifty-eight years old, she entered herself in the commercial directory as a *corsetière* for the last time.

From 1885 until 1898, then, Vuillard had lived with his family on or near the rue St. Honoré.[9] The atmosphere of the rue Daunou, where he had lived until 1885, was pervaded by the Opéra's public consumerism; the rue St. Honoré appears to have been dominated by the more old-world charm of the Tuileries.

A guidebook of 1884 describes the rue St. Honoré as having "an old entitlement of the bourgeoisie which stretches far back in the history of Paris."[10] The author of the book made specific reference to the particular prevalence of makers of luxury goods in the neighborhood:

> Merchants, principally drapers, furriers, embroiderers and those that sell rich stuffs or other *objets de luxe,* follow the example of the lordly personages who enrich them; behind the *hôtels* and the palaces of the nobles, this long rue St. Honoré flows like one of those grand rivers that traverse the whole of an empire, bringing it riches and fertility.[11]

From the author's discussion of the neighborhood surrounding the Vuillards' apartment, we can guess that Mme. Vuillard's business might have offered a convenient service to other merchants on her street:

> From the Protestant Oratory up to [the Church of] Saint Roch, the rue St. Honoré is more colorful, changeable, and luxurious. The commercial aristocrats here make themselves felt: they are mostly sellers of precious furs, of rich objects in gold, makers of clocks, and novelty shops.[12]

The author commented about the intersection of the rue St. Honoré and the rue d'Alger, which is the very corner where Vuillard lived between 1893 and 1897:

> We are almost forced to change pens: the old Paris ends here; no more merchants, no more commerce, no more ruins, all is new: mores, appearances, temples and palaces.[13]

In the direction of the Place Vendôme, the street "grows larger and draws attention by virtue of its splendor and its opulence."[14] Mme. Vuillard was situated in a location potentially advantageous to her business—at a boundary line between merchants and consumers. That the street had changed its personality is evident in the author's comment: "Although this immense street might still be famous for its commerce, it has lost much of its primitive character. . . . Alas! one finds there now only the upper middle class."[15]

Vuillard's interiors, as revealed in such works as *L'Atelier* or *The Vuillard Family at Lunch,* often look cramped, which adds much to the psychological tension that is evident in the paintings. The cluttered interior, however, was a commonplace of late

The Yellow Curtain

c. 1893

oil on canvas, 13¾ x 15⅜ inches,

National Gallery of Art, Washington,

D.C.; Ailsa Mellon Bruce Collection

nineteenth-century Paris. One therefore must distinguish between a typically crowded room that Vuillard might have recorded faithfully and his deliberate distortion, through exaggeration or reduction, of elements of an interior for decorative or psychological effect. In other words, the clutter and claustrophobia in his paintings may be either a result of Vuillard's pictorial distortion or a faithful depiction of a room furnished with a late nineteenth-century aesthetic. Do Vuillard's paintings reveal any reliable clues to what the interiors he depicted actually looked like, or did the interior serve merely as a private shorthand for Vuillard's feelings about the people he was portraying?

Contemporary photographs and periodicals reveal that at the end of the nineteenth century three primary decorative styles reigned in Parisian apartments.[16] The historicizing interior often included neo-Gothic or neo-Renaissance minstrels' galleries or suits of armor guarding immense fireplaces; its furnishings were intended to reflect the spirit of the France of the Valois or the Bourbon kings. In interiors decorated in the art nouveau style, which appeared at the end of the century, every element—from furniture and wall paneling to lamps and fabrics—conformed to a unified and modern aesthetic, without reference to a specific historical period. Finally, the eclectic interior—by far the most common of the three—was crowded with furnishings from many different periods; its walls were decorated with objets d'art ranging from paintings and mirrors to ceramic plates and woven tapestries, often hung over patterned wallpaper.

The historicizing interior, favored by the nouveaux riches, conformed to an aesthetic of grandeur whether the style being imitated were medieval, Renaissance, or ancien régime. In general, the style required the dimensions of an *hôtel particulier* to accommodate the necessary props; this style was widely derided by architectural purists, one of whom wrote:

> And how the function of older works is beautifully interpreted! You want to have exposed joists on your ceiling; but your joists are made out of cardboard paste, and since they might fall down if they projected too far, you have only half-joists. You'd like a monumental mantelpiece, but since it wasn't built along with the wall, its hood is too narrow and doesn't draw the smoke out. Furthermore, to avoid ruining the floor, your fireplace is reduced to a measly framework of wood or iron, coated in plaster, but painted and gilded. Your marble is stucco, your sculpture is pastry-cake, your windows are waxed paper. The upholsterer comes in and tops it all off with some banal hangings and a few gimrack pieces of furniture, and *voilà* what we have come to call art in the home.[17]

Critics saw the roots of this bad taste in society's lack of education and "its taste for *bibelots,* for fake archeology, its ignorance of the most elementary rules of artistic criticism . . . ":

> The imitation of a work of art is absurd, because it is impossible to encounter, in two different epochs, absolutely identical needs and ideas, requiring the same expression. But what is worse than imitation is the association, in a modern work, of bits borrowed from the works of different civilizations. What! not content to belong to the nineteenth century, you wish to bring together in your homes the porticoes of Pompei, the dining room of Henri II, the drawing room of Louis XIV and the boudoir of Louis XV?[18]

Indeed, this critic pleads for a unified aesthetic style, one that visually links all the elements in an interior and one whose visual manifestation relates to its function: "Every function can find a decorative expression; every work can take on a form that will determine its artistic character."[19]

During the 1890s, in reaction to the historicizing interior's excesses, the art nouveau aesthetic began to find a following in Paris. Instead of the medieval panoply or the crowded mixture of objects, the art nouveau style seemed at once pure and unified, based on undulating, "whiplash" lines, the adaptation of organic forms, and a unified architectural and decorative aesthetic based on abstraction.

Strikingly, examples of neither the historicizing nor the art nouveau interior appear in Vuillard's paintings. The scale and the grandeur required for the former are inconceivable in the interiors Vuillard painted in the 1890s, since the painter's own apartments, like the rooms in his paintings from these years, were small, their ceilings low, and their walls free of architectural embellishment. Even the large apartments of his friends, such as the home of Misia and Thadée Natanson on the rue

St. Florentin, were devoid of substantial architectural ornament. It is interesting, however, that Vuillard, who was at the forefront of artistic experimentation during this time, seems deliberately to have rejected the correspondingly avant-garde living environment of art nouveau, either for himself or for the interiors he painted.[20] That he preferred to surround himself with a jumble of accumulated objects remains interesting precisely because the sinuous lines in his work are often compared to decorative motifs in art nouveau and because his decorative commissions from the 1890s approach the interior as an organic whole.

All the same, though Vuillard may not have chosen—nor been able to afford—the high style of art nouveau for his apartments, he seems to have been aware of the art nouveau aesthetic. Similarities in pattern can be found between Vuillard's paintings and fabric designs of the art nouveau school, produced by such Parisian firms as Isaac between 1894 and 1897. For all their embrace of vegetal and organic forms and their interweaving of shapes, such designs tended to be simple. Most referred to flowers such as lilies and chrysanthemums or to animals such as birds and fish; forms were depicted with a minimal variety of colors. The vegetation typically was either a light color against a dark background or the reverse, but gradation in tone was rare and never were more than three colors applied. While some early designs from the Isaac studio seemed to recall Oriental landscapes, by 1897 the firm's designs were more abstract, evoking rather than depicting natural flora and fauna with flat tones and silhouetted shapes. Isaac created designs for a variety of uses: screens, curtains, tablecloths, dresses, and ladies' fans could be made from specialized models. Each design reflected its employment. A woman's dress might have flower stems growing from the hem and a light smattering of blossoms toward the waist and on the torso, while the pattern for a fan would reflect its semicircular shape.[21]

Although Vuillard's paintings at first might appear to employ complicated patterns, in fact the patterns in his paintings, like Isaac's, tend to be simple and straightforward, often composed of no more than two colors. It is, of course, the variety of the patterns and their juxtaposition that creates a dazzling and complicated effect. For example, *The Atelier* (see frontispiece), a study for one of the Desmarais decorations painted in 1892, shows several women in differently patterned dresses. The women are positioned parallel to the picture plane, as if in a frieze, and are shown against a background awash in pattern. The forms of the fabrics themselves are not organic in the same way as Isaac's, but their overall disposition on the canvas presages the sinuous lines of art nouveau.

In spite of their stylistic affinities with the emerging art nouveau style, however, Vuillard's paintings almost always represent at the most ordinary level the eclectic interiors of the last quarter of the nineteenth century, rooms furnished with a style of decoration particulary favored by the Parisian bourgeoisie of the 1890s. This aesthetic valued the jumbled, mismatched assemblage of objects: "For the kind of decoration considered elegant in the last part of the century," as one author put it, "only the words bric-a-brac or junk seem appropriate terms."[22]

Throughout his career, Vuillard chose to live in and to paint rooms like these. They can be seen in photographs from humble city apartments to country chateaux, from bourgeois dwellings to aristocratic homes. Interior decoration in this style was also much derided by contemporary critics who castigated the citizenry for embracing an architectural and decorative style completely incompatible with the needs of modern life.[23]

Vuillard's friend Claude Anet, for whom he painted a series of decorations, in 1897 published an article on modern decoration in *The Architectural Record* under his pseudonym Jean Schopfer. He argued that:

> The nineteenth century will leave no landmark in the history of decoration and the arts of ornamentation. Modern society has, so far, been unable to create or to furnish and embellish its dwelling in an original style. . . . Hardly ever will one find an article made for the new purpose which it has to serve. We live on the past. . . . Thus, an examination of our apartments would lead to the following discouraging conclusion: that modern society, confused and divided, has not yet succeeded in forming an idea of its tastes and requirements, and that, finding it impossible to discover any new form of decoration, it is reduced to living, so to speak, in other people's houses, and to reviving in its own behalf furniture and decorations made for other circles, and which were perfect only because they correspond to the needs and taste of their day.[24]

Another theorist, lamenting the lack of a unified aesthetic style for interior decoration, attributed its cause to changing social and economic patterns, especially to France's difficult transition from monarchy to democracy. He stated that in a monarchy style typically filtered down from the king to the people but that in a democracy the route was from the bottom to the top. The rapidly changing social structure in late nineteenth-century France had created situations in which people did not settle in one house for life but instead were constantly moving from one rented apartment to another.[25]

Vuillard's various moves throughout his life attest to this phenomenon of social fluidity and constant change. And the sense of crowding that one feels upon looking at his paintings of interiors certainly reflects the sensibilities described by these critics. Nonetheless, Vuillard's paintings remain an ambiguous record of what his living environment actually looked like, leaving the viewer with a much stronger sense of the rooms' feeling than of their appearance.

To guess what Vuillard's apartments really looked like, we might study descriptions of their size and their context within neighborhoods or compare photographs Vuillard took with his painted works. One pair of photographs (figs. 47 and 48), taken by Vuillard in the apartment on the rue Truffaut where he lived from 1899 until 1904, shows family and friends gathered around the dining table (for a discussion of this apartment, see page 94). Although the tablecloth is the same in both pictures, the angle is slightly different in each, and it is not clear if the photographs were taken at the same meal. In the photograph of the right side of the room (fig. 48), only one lamp is on the table, and three of the four people can be identified clearly: his mother is to the right in the foreground, Pierre Herman is next to her, and Marthe Mellot (who was married to Thadée's brother Alfred Natanson) is across from him. In the other picture (fig. 47) a different woman sits in the left foreground, there are two lamps on the table (although one might have been moved to improve the composition of Vuillard's previous photograph), and a bottle of white wine has been added. Regardless of these discrepancies, however, the wallpaper, curtains, and pictures on the walls indicate that the two photographs were taken in the same room.

The wallpaper is a small geometric pattern of a type that was in vogue at the end of the century.[26] The curtains hang straight down from the top of the window, which was also typical of the time, as were the lace curtains that hung directly over the glass. The small plates on the wall above Mme. Vuillard's head and on the other side of the room were standard elements of wall decoration. This apartment clearly differed from the average Parisian dwelling because of the paintings, mostly un-framed, that covered most of the walls—characteristic of an artist's establishment. One of these paintings, the *Portrait of the Artist's Grandmother* (fig. 49), is readily identifiable as it hangs in the corner of the room, wedged between window and wall.

A painting of Mme. Vuillard sewing (fig. 50) shows the same room during the day. The table appears to have been moved away from the window, although Vuillard's vantage point in the photograph might have distorted its relative position to the window. It has also been covered with a paisley shawl, a standard decorating device. The chairs have been lined up against the chair rail on both sides of the room. In short, the purpose of the room has shifted from eating to working.

Vuillard's painting of the room shows many of the same decorations visible in the photographs but with fewer paintings, which gives the impression of a greater formality. Instead of showing several unframed canvases hanging on a wall or tacked to the wallpaper, Vuillard painted one horizontal, framed picture hanging above the chairs. The plates above and beside the door remain, however, as do the paintings that flank the window. The picture to the right of the window, distinguished by its large frame, is clearly the same in both the photograph and the painting, but where the photograph identifies the picture as Vuillard's portrait of his grandmother, the picture's subject has been obscured in the painting. The dining room table is clear of both food and wine, with plates, glasses, and bottles presumably returned to the kitchen. Other items, such as the lamps, however, would have been removed from the table and placed on the tall chest of drawers after each meal. It is therefore likely that the dark shadow that appears to be an element of the framed picture but does not fit logically as the silhouette of the grandmother is in fact a lamp shade that Vuillard cut off at the same line as the picture frame. This is a typical Vuillardian device, one he had used to great effect as early as 1893 in *Interior with Chiffonnier* (fig. 54), where the lamp is also placed on top of the bureau, casting a ghostly light on Vuillard's mother and leaving Vuillard's sister in darkness.

The chest that we see in both the photograph and the painting of 1899 of the

dining room on the rue Truffaut also plays an important role in other paintings by Vuillard, most significantly in the 1893 painting of his mother and sister (see fig. 55). In this painting the chest is placed against the wall directly behind Vuillard's mother. Although the photograph reveals it to be a tall dresser, it looms even larger in this painting because of the skewed perspective with a vanishing point near the top drawer. Vuillard also slanted the top of the bureau so that the viewer can see it, creating an irrational sense of space with the steep upward angle of the floor. The chest establishes Mme. Vuillard as the focal element of the picture. A green baize cloth visible in this canvas on the top of the piece would have been placed there to protect the surface from scratching when items from the table were returned there after the meals were finished.

While not of a particularly distinguished design, the dresser nonetheless was made of mahogany and destined for a public room.[27] In marked contrast is the dresser in the 1899 painting *Woman Sweeping* (fig. 51), which is made of a blond wood. Although furniture constructed from this kind of wood normally was reserved for private rooms, the chest of drawers was part of the dining room furniture in the Vuillards' apartment on the rue Truffaut. The woman is sweeping the same room that Vuillard depicted in the picture of his mother sewing (see fig. 50): the wallpaper is the same and a shawl covers the table in both scenes.

A different view of the dining room on the rue Truffaut is the subject of another painting, *The Breakfast Table (Madame Vuillard, rue Truffaut)* (fig. 52), in which the table is set for a meal. The blond dresser here has, inexplicably, nine rather than

47

Left: Photograph by Vuillard of the left side of a room in Vuillard's apartment on the rue Truffaut, c. 1899–1901. Archives Antoine Salomon, Paris

Right: Photograph by Vuillard of the right side of a room in Vuillard's apartment on the rue Truffaut, c. 1899–1901. Archives Antoine Salomon, Paris

49 ❧

Portrait of the Artist's

Grandmother

c. 1891–92

oil on canvas, 25⅝ x 21¼ inches,

Hirshhorn Museum and Sculpture Garden,

Smithsonian Institution; gift of Marion L.

Ring estate, 1987

50

Interior with Woman Sewing

1899

oil on canvas, 20¾ x 19½ inches, The

Metropolitan Museum of Art, New York;

Robert Lehman Collection, 1975

eight drawers, but the plate above the door is the same as in the painting of Mme. Vuillard sewing. In all of these pictures, Vuillard made the room seem quite large and square, when in the photographs it seems small and narrow.

Through photographs we can identify various elements of Vuillard's actual interiors in his work. From this we can conclude that the specific objects themselves do not create the claustrophobic atmosphere of the paintings. Vuillard's sensibility for the interior, therefore, is twofold. His lush combinations of pigment and pattern vividly evoke late nineteenth-century Parisian life in paintings that depict the crowded rooms of fin-de-siècle France. Because they express more what the rooms felt like than how they appeared, however, Vuillard's interiors are most effective as metaphors, speaking for the relationships between the people who occupy them, as well as for Vuillard himself and for the feelings he wanted to convey.

A study of the actuality of Vuillard's places of residence is particularly important because paintings of his family, chiefly his mother, constitute the largest body of his artistic production. The actual interiors of these family pictures, though often not specifically described, are central to the compositions, for it was in these rooms that

51 ❧

Woman Sweeping

c. 1899

oil on cardboard, 18 x 19 inches,

The Phillips Collection, Washington,

D.C.

76

52 ❧

The Breakfast Table (Madame Vuillard, rue Truffaut)

1900

oil on cardboard, 15½ x 22¾ inches,

Staatsgalerie Stuttgart

the psychological dramas evolved. By using facts about changes in the Vuillard family's economic status, and more importantly, the differences between the real and the painted interior, one can draw conclusions about Vuillard's methods of pictorial interpretation.

Initial comparisons by other scholars of photographs of Vuillard's apartments and his paintings yielded numerous insights into Vuillard's manipulation of the interior for expressive meaning. Such comparisons must be made cautiously, however, to allow for the distortion of the photographic lens. Comparing one distorted form with another does not lead to clear understanding of the actual interior space.[28] The layout and appearance of the apartments themselves, crucial to our understanding of Vuillard's choices for the interior views he painted, are something neither his photographs nor his paintings reveal.

In the journals Vuillard does not address directly how he translated the actual elements of a given room into a tightly woven composition. But in an interesting passage, written in 1894, one can observe how Vuillard's imagination moved from the natural environment around him to an edited, internally arranged pictorial translation. This passage is so important to reach an understanding of Vuillard's way of seeing and thinking about the interior that it will be quoted in full:

> On the table at noon the chrysanthemums, violet and white. An ornamental motif that is at once serious and pleasing. Decoration for a desk. Flowers after all are a common, simple ornament, I don't mean to say that I scorn them, but they don't demand much effort to grasp their appearance, their forms and colors, it's properly the true natural ornament. Their ornamental sense is primitive, simple, interesting enough in the quality of their forms and colors; quite on the contrary a painting, which is also made up of forms and colors, demands of the spirit that contemplates it a more complex effort of the imagination. For other objects—a figure, a pot, for example—their ornamental interest is less brutal, there are no vivid colors, no multiple repetition of like forms (like petals). What danger there is in attaching more importance to ideas than to the cause that gives birth to them. And how natural it is to me in my weakness always to fall into that trap. Thus this idea of the life surrounding us, of our life, source of all our thoughts and productions, this becomes modernism (paintings of interiors, in the sense of [my] journal) a commonplace the comprehension of which becomes as foggy as the others.
>
> This morning in my bed upon wakening I was looking at the different objects that surrounded me, the ceiling painted white, the ornament in the middle, vaguely 18th-century arabesques, the mirrored armoire opposite, the grooves, the molding of the woodwork, of the window, their proportions, the *curtains,* the chair in front of them with its back of carved wood, the paper on the wall, the knobs of the open door, glass and copper, the wood of the bed, the wood of the screen, the hinges, my clothes at the foot of the bed; the four elegant green leaves in a pot, the inkwell, the books, the curtains of the other window, the walls of the court through it, the differences of perspective through the two windows, one with a little patch of sky parallel to the window, in the other, making a perpendicular angle, the impression that results from only that corner. . . . When it comes to the curtains, differences and patterns obtained by the greater or lesser spacing of the threads. Comparing the qualities of each of these objects to that alone I feel pleased. Then I was struck by the abundance of ornament in all these objects. They are what one calls in bad taste and if they were not familiar to me they might be unbearable. It's a chance to think about this label "in bad taste" that I am quick to say and that keeps me from looking. There I was looking and nothing gave my nerves a shock on the surface, I took interest in each of their qualities, and that was enough to push away distaste. One mustn't stray into these impressions of a "little master," as one might have said once; try on the contrary to understand the character [of objects]; it's just as difficult, even more so, I think, but very instructive, to understand a vulgar thing (I don't mean simple), a common thing, as it is to understand a sanctioned thing that has moved you. To thus understand the world was, I believe, the goal originally pointed out by those who first spoke of the modern and of modernity. They were sure of finding in this [kind of] sincere and unprejudiced study grand emotions and subjects sometimes grand and not always ridiculous. The ridiculous is something perhaps just as tormenting and depressing for the spirit that feels it and points it out in others as it is for those that are its victims. By feeling so much the ridiculous, one ends up being unable to fix his attention on anything. Truly this morning the result of all these observations wasn't distaste, [but] an acceptance that, if stronger, might have given me even more fertile

ideas. And another thing, in the middle of all these objects, I was astonished to see Mama enter in a blue peignoir with white stripes. To sum up, not one of these inanimate objects had any simple ornamental connection with another, the whole was as disparate as possible. All the same there was a vivid atmosphere, and it gave off an impression that was not at all disagreeable. The arrival of Mama was surprising—a living person. For the painter, the differences of shapes, of forms, were interest enough.[29]

This extended reflection on the nature of vision, aesthetics, and the emotional power of observation is surely among the most cogently argued and thoughtful of Vuillard's journal entries. Vuillard's initial observation of the world around him, a vase of flowers, a bureau, his bedroom, is extremely careful and minute, "without prejudice." He draws special attention to the optical effects created by his point of vantage, lying in the bed, which results in different perceptions of the pattern of the curtains. Similarly, he takes note of the windows' perspectival shifts, the changing aspect of the world outside his room, that his unusual point of view occasions. The complexities of pattern and decoration resulting from different perspectives and perceptions are often the focal point of his compositions. Vuillard reveals in this passage his pleasure in the purely optical, abstract character of the environment, most effectively captured without reference to the function or associative values of objects. This calculatedly naive vision permits the artist to observe his environment without recourse to conventional artistic rules; conventional representation of space, for instance, becomes less important to him than the two-dimensional pattern observed by his eye, the "ornamental value" of the things he looks at. This discovery of the affective power of naive vision may have given rise to Vuillard's propensity for depicting several perspectives in one painting, to give a more total impression of the environment by reflecting different perspectival orientations as his shifting gaze resulted in a similarly changing point of view.

Nowhere in Vuillard's art is this device more evident than in the *Large Interior with Six Figures* (fig. 53), a work unique in the artist's oeuvre. Despite its unusually large size, unparalleled in Vuillard's conventional pictures, this work, as far as can be established, was not painted on commission and was not intended for any decorative function. The scale of the painting, almost six feet wide, relates it to the decorative series Vuillard painted for the Desmarais family, Dr. Vasquez (these panels are now at the Petit Palais, Paris), and the Natansons (see "The Music of Painting"). But its compositional complexity, the placement of its figures, and its highly sophisticated colorism link this work to the most complex of Vuillard's easel paintings. The work's subject matter, moreover, excludes it from consideration as a work painted on commission for a client, for Vuillard never painted for hire the intimate interiors that were the domain of his family and closest friends, turning instead to more conventional subjects, such as landscape painting.

In the *Large Interior with Six Figures*, Vuillard shows a remarkably complex space, viewed with the calculatedly naive eye. At left, seated in an upholstered chair, is Mme. Vuillard; facing her, with her back turned to the viewer, is a woman who

53

Large Interior with Six

Figures

1897

Overleaf: oil on canvas, 35⅜ x 76⅜

inches, Kunsthaus Zürich

might be Marie. In the center of the canvas is a couple whose identity remains unclear; the identities of the two other figures, a woman in the distant background and a bending woman at the right margin of the canvas, also remain a mystery. Although the figures occupy the same canvas surface, they do not necessarily occupy a unified space—a space with a consistent logic of perspective and spatial representation. The foreground figure spans almost the entire height of the composition, and yet the table on which she leans advances farther into the viewer's space. Although she addresses Mme. Vuillard, she overwhelms the seated figure in scale and further dwarfs the couple beside her. The painter's shifting point of view, turning from side to side in a series of panoramic views, isolates each figure or group of figures in his or her own discrete space.

Patterned objects play a significant role in structuring the composition. In 1894, while looking at his room full of eighteenth-century style embellishments, Vuillard had been struck at first by its "bad taste." But when he looked carefully at each isolated object, paying attention to its individual character, he could then go beyond a hasty critique to a more telling judgment. That beauty may inhere in a common object, Vuillard had written, is one of the seminal ideas of modernism—that art need no longer be based on beautiful things. The challenge for the artist is not to bring out the beauty of an obviously lovely object like a flower—"the sanctified object that has moved you"—but to penetrate the inherent character of a table or a curtain, and to discover in it a thing of beauty.

Vuillard seemed to argue that objects in themselves were potent as physical forms, without the labels or judgments that humanity brought to them. The whole scene lacked focus, however, until his mother arrived in a blue and white striped robe. Vuillard's rumination on the character of objects built up to this sudden apparition, which seemed to bring the whole scene together into a lively composition of colors, forms, and lines.

In the *Large Interior with Six Figures,* complicated patterns of the rugs, layered one on top of another, contribute to the painting's overall sense of disconnected continuity. Vuillard had used this device in some of his earlier decorations, but here the overwhelming spatiality of the composition makes the patterns of the carpets convey the painting's mood of psychological disjunction. Color, too, is an important component of the work's emotional range, inasmuch as Vuillard has stressed, in tones of infinite variety, the dominant note of red throughout the composition. Although the six figures coexist in this hermetically sealed environment—like characters in a Symbolist play—they nonetheless occupy their own sectors, each represented in a different scale, as if in a different world.

The notion that an object takes on a particular appearance when seen from a certain point of view and a certain state of mind is at the center of Vuillard's approach to the depiction of a particular space. Tied to this notion is the idea that viewpoint and perspective can be used for expressive purposes—to heighten perception of emotion, for example. In an extraordinary composition, *Woman in Blue* (fig. 58), Vuillard manipulated spatial distortion to a degree unprecedented in his art. Dated 1893, the painting shows a corner of the dining room from the apartment on the rue St. Honoré that is dominated by the strip of windows at the top of the wall. A figure, almost certainly Marie, seated in the nearest plane of the composition, looks over her shoulder toward the viewer, although her eyes are cast in shadow. Her arm rests on the back of a chair and spans the canvas. In the space formed by the crook of her arm, another figure can be discerned beneath the windows. Although the two figures are only separated by a table width, the difference in their size is extreme and can only be accounted for in perspectival terms by the proximity of Vuillard to the foreground figure. The disquieting physical aspects of this composition, such as the discrepancies of scale, along with its peculiar psychological tension, can thus be attributed to the painter's point of view.

One of Vuillard's most compelling paintings is the claustrophobic *Mother and Sister of the Artist* (fig. 55). Vuillard's mother in a black dress sits squarely in a chair in front of a bureau, while his sister on the left seems to disappear into the wallpaper. The exaggerated perspective—the floor appears to rise and the walls to close in—creates an air of intense congestion that is exacerbated by the painting's small size. This painting is an extension of the psychological drama shown in other paintings of the Vuillard family at a meal. Since a table—the only element in the room other than the two figures and the chest—with a plate, napkin, and wine bottle is just visible, one can read the scene as taking place after the meal has finished.

The placement of the figures in this painting does much to stress their objective ornamental character. Vuillard manipulated the pattern of Marie's plaid dress to reinforce its decorative flatness and to eliminate any sense of the body underneath. The horizontal lines of the dress continue across uninterrupted, while the vertical lines in the pattern negate the extreme foreshortening of the figure. The abrupt cropping of the silhouette, especially around the shoulders, also increases the visual blending of the dress into the wallpaper. Marie, awkwardly bent over, appears to be struggling to remain within the shrinking confines of the picture, which have been determined by the painter's unusual choice of point of view.[30] The bottom corner of the window seems to press her further down. Although there is no place for Marie's feet on the baseboard, the mother rests solidly on her large foot.[31] The contrast between the two figures is extreme: the mother in black sitting securely and seen head on, and the daughter fading into the background, bent over and ephemeral.

Vuillard returned again and again to the theme of mother and daughter, almost always with a measure of tension. In such works as *Interior with Chiffonnier* (see fig. 54), *The Chat (La Causette)* (fig. 57), and *Mother and Sister of the Artist* (fig. 56), Vuillard explored variations on the perplexing theme of his mother's dominance and his sister's submission. In each painting Mme. Vuillard is shown comfortably seated and frontally posed. Marie, by contrast, seems to shrink from contact, avoiding the

83

54

Interior with Chiffonnier

1893

oil on canvas, 18¹⁄₆ x 15 inches,

Kunstmuseum Winterthur, Switzerland

viewer's eye. Is it possible to conclude that these paintings reflect an unpleasant, even agonizing, relationship between mother and daughter?

One must search in vain for an explanation of this relationship in Vuillard's journal. It is perhaps telling that Vuillard, when recording his most personal thoughts, wrote nothing about the tension that the modern-day observer senses in these paintings. It is true that many of the mother-daughter paintings were painted before 1893, when Vuillard first began to record more intimate observations about his personal life. At that time, too, Marie left the household to marry Roussel. Still, she was in Mme. Vuillard's apartment on a daily basis as a worker.

In a pair of paintings, *Breakfast* (fig. 59) and *Le Chocolat (Breakfast)* (fig. 60), depicting two figures having coffee that seems related to his mother-daughter images, Vuillard focused on the background figure, who stares directly out toward the viewer; in a related painting, *Two Women Drinking Coffee* (fig. 61), he chose to focus directly on the foreground figure. It is difficult to determine, however, whether these are depictions of Mme. Vuillard and Marie. Although the dress of the rear figure in *Le Chocolat* is the same worn by Marie in many other pictures, the face appears older than one would expect. Instead of the tunnel-like perspective of *Mother and Sister of the Artist* (see fig. 55), we see in these pictures, which depict the same room, neither the ceiling nor the floor, and the window ledge, so ominous and crushing in the former work, is depicted here almost parallel to the picture plane. The chest frames Marie this time, not Mme. Vuillard, but it serves more as a cloth of honor than the looming heavy presence that one senses from the earlier painting.[32] The breadth of wall between window and chest and between chest and door provides a breathing space. Thus Vuillard's change in point of view renders a less claustrophobic environment and a greater sense of calm, even though all three pictures portray the same characters and the same room.

Yet another pair of paintings enlarges on the mother-daughter drama. In *The*

55

Mother and Sister of the

Artist

c. 1893

oil on canvas, 18¼ x 22¼ inches,

The Museum of Modern Art, New York;

gift of Mrs. Saidie A. May

56 ❧

Mother and Sister of the Artist

1892

Top left: oil on cardboard, 8¼ x 9½ inches, Collection S.

58 ❧

Woman in Blue

1893

Opposite: oil on panel, 10½ x 8¾ inches, private collection

57 ❧

The Chat (La Causette)

c. 1892

Bottom left: oil on canvas, 12¾ x 16¼ inches, Scottish National Gallery of Modern Art, Edinburgh

Dressmakers from 1892 (fig. 64), Mme. Vuillard stands erect on the right side of the canvas, her dress of brown and black vertical stripes reinforcing her solid frame. A table covered with a pile of different materials separates her from Marie, who hovers in the background and appears to fade into the wall behind her. Her face is devoid of features, and the midsection of her dress forms a void with the same tone of neutral green as the wall, emblematic of her lost center or identity. The view through the trellised window appears flat, a tableau rather than a refreshing outlet to the natural world. Although the sunlight that filters through the window highlights some of the material on the table and allows some of Mme. Vuillard's features to be seen, for the most part the two figures remain in shadow. Mme. Vuillard's stolid pose is reinforced by the vertical line of the closed shutter, while Marie's bent form is echoed in the curves of the curtain on the side of the nearby window. The women appear to be locked in confrontation, facing each other across an untraversable divide.

A similar juxtaposition can be seen in *The Conversation* (fig. 62). Here Mme. Vuillard is seated squarely in the foreground with her head turned in profile to Marie, who hovers behind a table while holding a chair as if fending off a maternal assault. Marie is framed by the triangular shape of a curtain in the right and by a figure in a patterned dress in the background. Her ghostlike pallor and skeletal features recall the faces in Edvard Munch's paintings from the mid-1890s.[33]

These two compositions are anticipated by two drawings from Vuillard's program for Maurice Maeterlinck's play *The Intruder,* performed at the Théâtre de l'Art in May 1891 (see fig. 63).[34] On the back of a drawing now in the collection of the Bibliothèque Nationale, Vuillard had written "le rideau des arts." Both drawings show one figure in the foreground peeking out from behind a curtain and another

59 🐦

Breakfast

c. 1893

Left: oil on cardboard, 12 x 12½ inches,

William Kelly Simpson

Le Chocolat (Breakfast)

c. 1893

Opposite, right: oil on wood panel, 13⅛ x

15⅛ inches, Rose Art Museum, Brandeis

University, Waltham, Massachusetts;

gift of Mr. and Mrs. Albert Dreitzer,

New York

figure sitting in the background on a chair. The composition is divided along a diagonal from upper left to lower right, so the space appears both to recede dramatically and to remain flat. There is no shading to indicate depth; only the opening of the curtain suggests a piercing of the picture plane. Vuillard depicted these scenes with the most minimal of means—a black ink wash—and used the most primitive method of creating depth: the figure who sits in the chair appears to be in the background because she is higher up on the picture plane. She blends into the wall in much the same way as Marie does in *The Dressmakers,* and she wears a similar dress. In the painting the diamond-shaped patterns in the bodice of the dress blend into the background; Vuillard achieved this effect in the drawings by leaving the torso blank.

George Mauner linked the two figures to the Symbolist expressions of the dual nature of life and of the manifestations of spiritual aspects of life in ordinary daily existence.[35] Although these pictures do not illustrate directly the plot of *The Intruder,* which focuses on Death taking away a mother and her newborn child, they nonetheless use motifs taken from the play to infuse everyday life with drama. For example, the only character in the play that can perceive the presence of the figure of Death is the child's grandfather, who is blind. The plot of the play thus reflected the Symbolist belief that inner sight, despite its distortions, is more perceptive than observation—a belief shared by Vuillard, in spite of his dependence on the observed motif.

This idea was common to the Symbolist artists with whom Vuillard associated—

61 ❦

Two Women Drinking Coffee

1891

oil on cardboard, 8½ x 11⅜ inches,

National Gallery of Art, Washington,

D.C.; Ailsa Mellon Bruce Collection

to his friend Odilon Redon, for example, whose *Les Yeux clos* of 1890 depicts a figure with closed eyes, indicative of the heightened awareness of his inner spirit.[36] Vuillard's paintings express a similar air of mystery and of inner understanding not through such anecdotal symbology but through their distortions of pictorial space.

In 1895 Vuillard produced a lithograph, *Le Déjeuner,* that evoked the mystery often associated by the painter with the rituals at the end of a meal (fig. 66). A young woman, possibly Marie, sits in the foreground with her arm resting on the table and nurses a cup of coffee. She gazes somewhat wistfully out of the picture in the direction of the viewer. Two figures behind her, the farther one resembling Vuillard's mother, are clearing the table. The reflective expression of the foreground figure may indicate simply a postprandial reverie, but Vuillard instilled a further air of mystery by positioning the woman to take up the entire width of the page, her torso lined up against the left side and her skirt and arm extending to the right. Thus, like *Woman in Blue,* she dominates the entire foreground space and is removed both physically and psychologically from the people behind her. Vuillard has reinforced this isolation by depicting the foreground figure in detail while barely sketching in the figures in the background using smudged and scratched crayon. The middle figure, seen from the back, forms a light halo around the woman in the foreground and a stark white silhouette against the dark wall behind.

The composition of this lithograph is similar to that of *Intimité*, a much more emotionally fraught lithograph from about the same time.[37] Vuillard creates a claustrophobic space for the three figures with strange lighting, which comes from at least two sources outside of the picture, with a buildup of figures and patterned screens and walls that induce a feeling of *horror vacuii,* as there are no untouched surfaces where the eye can rest, and with several points of view in the same picture. The frenetic activity of his scratching on the lithographic stone produces bizarre highlights for the composition.

62

The Conversation

1891

Left: oil on canvas, 9⅜ x 13⅛ inches,

National Gallery of Art, Washington,

D.C.; Ailsa Mellon Bruce Collection

63

Right: Drawing from Maeterlinck's The

Intruder, 1891, brush and india ink on

paper, 7½ x 10 inches, private collection,

New York

64 ✺

The Dressmakers

1892

oil on canvas, 9½ x 13 inches, from the

Private Collection of Jane Forbes Clark,

New York

For Vuillard the table was a place of drama. He often painted his family or close friends gathered together for a meal, using tightly woven compositions to capitalize on the interrelationships, tension, and psychological isolation of the people involved. Even when only a single person is highlighted, as in *Le Déjeuner,* he seeks to establish a sense of wistfulness, an almost alienated mood. In works such as two paintings entitled *Breakfast* (figs. 65 and 67) or *Madame Vuillard at the Table* (fig. 68), by manipulating his compositions to a great extent and allowing furniture, such as the dining table or a chest of drawers, to dominate people, Vuillard enhanced this feeling of psychological distance.

In 1898 Vuillard's family life underwent a distinct change. His mother retired from the corset business after twenty years of directing her atelier. As a consequence she and her son moved from the neighborhood of the rue St. Honoré into an apartment

65 ❧

Breakfast

1892

oil on cardboard, 12⅛ x 10½ inches,

private collection, Rochester, New York

66

Le Déjeuner

c. 1895

lithograph, 9⅞ x 6⁵⁄₁₆ inches, as

reproduced in Roger-Marx, L'Oeuvre gravé

de Vuillard, no. 15

67 ❧

Breakfast

1894

oil on cardboard mounted on wood, 10⅝ x

9 inches, National Gallery of Art,

Washington, D.C.; Ailsa Mellon Bruce

Collection

68 ❧

Madame Vuillard at the

Table

c. 1895

oil on canvas, 13½ x 16½ inches,

the collection of Janice H. Levin

69 ✦

The Roussel Family at

Dinner

1894–95

Left: oil on canvas, 19½ x 25½ inches,

Josefowitz Collection

70 ✦

Annette's Lunch

1900

Right: oil on cardboard, 13⅞ x 24⅜

inches, Musée de l'Annonciade,

Saint-Tropez

near the Place Clichy, altogether a different quarter of Paris. The neighborhood had been noted since the middle of the century for its artists and literati and was no less lively than the commercial district that the Vuillards had inhabited since the 1870s. By 1899 the painter and his mother were installed in a modest apartment at 28, rue Truffaut—the apartment pictured in the photographs of friends and family dining.

This is the only apartment that exists today in the same form as when Vuillard lived in it. The apartment is modest in scale, with small rooms feeding into one another. The low ceilings and the absence of connecting hallways give the space a simple, essentially humble character. On the other hand, because the apartment is set back from the street, sunlight filters through the windows at both front and back, giving the rooms a sense of light and cheerfulness. The move to the rue Truffaut may, therefore, have contributed to the change that Vuillard's painting underwent in the last years of the decade. But another event in the Vuillard family's life seems to have had a more lasting effect on Vuillard's interior scenes: the birth in 1898 of his niece Annette Roussel.

The paintings of the early 1890s that show Mme. Vuillard and Marie suggest deep tensions in the relationship between mother and daughter through the airless interplay of skewed perspective and overlapping pattern. Marie's marriage to Roussel did not do much to bring happiness to the household; Vuillard records "complications in the Roussel household" in his chronology for 1895. Paintings such as *Married Life*

72 ❧

Mother and Child

c. 1900

oil on cardboard, 20¼ x 19¾ inches,

Herbert Black, Canada

73 ❧

The Newspaper

c. 1895

oil on cardboard, 13½ x 21¾ inches,

The Phillips Collection, Washington,

D.C.

Figure at a Window

c. 1892

oil on board on panel, 12⅝ x 9⅞ inches,

private collection, New York

(c. 1894, private collection),³⁸ where the figure of a man and a woman, almost certainly Marie and Roussel, are isolated from each other at opposite ends of a room, attest to the strains on this relationship. *The Roussel Family at Dinner* (fig. 69), with its garish artificial light that throws Roussel and a companion into melancholy shadow, likewise suggests that all was not happy with the Roussels at first. With the birth of Annette, however, a sense of peace and happiness came over the family. For Vuillard, this is reflected in a new series of images of mothers and daughters, which have none of the tortured overtones of the pictures he painted of Mme. Vuillard and Marie from 1890 to 1893.

Often Vuillard paints his mother, for him the principal image of maternity, with the baby Annette. Paintings that show Mme. Vuillard feeding her granddaughter, such as *Annette's Lunch* (fig. 70), demonstrate the degree to which the anxious sentiment of the earlier paintings has been dispelled. The paintings of Mme. Vuillard and Marie often revolved around a meal, but their psychological disconnection represented the antithesis of the meal's nourishing implications. Here, though only an infant, Annette appears to look directly at her grandmother, while the painting's warm palette and gentle patterning reflect the altogether brighter mood of the household.

Annette is shown at about the same age in two paintings, *Child in a Room* (fig. 71) and *Mother and Child* (fig. 72), that Vuillard probably painted in one room of his own apartment on the rue Truffaut. In both paintings Annette wears a smocked dress with a red collar. Vuillard pays particular attention to his niece's small gestures and her tiny rounded form, leaving the rest of the room in a comparative haze. Dramatic distortions of scale, like dramatic effects of light and shadow, are usually absent from these works: Vuillard bathes his subject in the warmth of his evident contentment.

The paintings of Marie with her daughter also add a new dimension to Vuillard's paintings of the interior, with the inclusion of windows giving a view to the out of doors. Windows were by no means absent from Vuillard's earlier pictures, yet in his paintings from the first half of the 1890s these windows give little sense of light and air. *Figure at a Window* (fig. 74), for example, a work painted about 1892, reduces all elements to flat solid forms. *L'Atelier* and *L'Aiguillée* from 1893, or the painting *The Newspaper* (fig. 73) from about the same time, offer views from windows, and *Madame*

98

Vuillard by the Window (fig. 75) and *Marie Vuillard at Her Window* (fig. 76), both from about 1893, show the familiar figures of Vuillard's world looking out from their apartment. In none of these, however, does Vuillard concern himself with giving a sense of the atmospheric differences between the interior and the exterior. Although windows are shown, the view through them is usually as dense and as solid as the rooms in which the figures reside.

At the end of the century Vuillard opened up this view, and in *At the Window* (fig. 78), he showed his niece as a toddler leaning over the window sill to look at the landscape beyond. Marie, dwarfing her daughter in scale, is enveloped in the shadows of the room, barely visible as a watchful maternal presence at right. In another painting, *Child at a Window* (fig. 77), Vuillard again emphasized his niece's tiny form

76 ❧

Marie Vuillard at Her

Window

c. 1893

oil on board, 12⅝ x 11 inches,

Beverly Sommer, New York

by placing it against a much larger shape—in this case the tall frame of a French window. She is shown from the outside looking into the apartment, though perhaps from another room across the courtyard.

This was a novelty for Vuillard, who almost never showed the members of his immediate family in the open air. The sense of privacy that is central to his paintings

77 ❧

Child at a Window

1901

oil on cardboard, 13⁹/₁₆ x 10¹/₁₆ inches,

courtesy of Dumbarton Oaks Research

Library and Collection, Washington, D.C.

At the Window

c. 1900

oil on canvas, 19⅛ x 24⅜ inches, San

Francisco Museum of Modern Art; partial

gift of Mrs. Wellington S. Henderson

of his family and closest friends found its pictorial analogy in the tightly woven spaces and patterns of the interior. With his paintings of Annette, a new freedom made its way into his art. His condensed pictorial spaces were opened up to the out of doors, if only by means of a landscape seen through an open window.

But more important, Vuillard's subject matter changed significantly around 1900. While his family still served him as a model in the early decades of the twentieth century, Vuillard moved more and more in the world of fashion and artistic circles outside the confines of his mother's apartment. As a painter of society portraits and decorations, he moved into a brighter, bigger world, leaving the dark and intimate interiors of his family behind him.

THE MUSIC OF PAINTING:

HOMAGES TO MISIA

Who speaks of art speaks of poetry. There is no art without a poetic aim.

There is a species of emotion particular to painting. There is an effect that

results from a certain arrangement of colors, of lights, of shadows, etc.

79

Misia and Thadée Natanson

It is this that one calls the music of painting.

c. 1897

EV I.2, 68 (January 1894)

oil on paper mounted on canvas, 41 x 28

inches, private collection; photograph

courtesy of Acquavella Galleries, New York

*M*isia Natanson, the woman who in addition to his mother was the muse of Vuillard's early years, was the central character in a group of paintings that date from the end of the 1890s. Misia was the only figure outside of his family whom Vuillard painted again and again during the decade. These pictures not only pay tribute to her musical talent—she was an accomplished pianist—but also record the unrequited emotions Vuillard felt for her and could express only in painting.

The paintings of Misia Natanson mark a shift away from the private intimacy of his family life to the worldly society that revolved around the *Revue Blanche.* Founded in Belgium in 1889 and published in Paris from 1891 to 1903 by Thadée Natanson with his brothers Alfred and Alexandre, the journal was one of many created at the end of the century, such as *La Plume, L'Occident, La Mercure de France,* and *La Revue Wagnérienne,* to take advantage of the new intellectual vitality in literature and in art. The *Revue Blanche* vowed to be "open to all opinions and schools" of thought—thus the inspiration for its title, which saw in the color white the sum of all colors.[1]

The offices of the *Revue Blanche* on the rue des Martyrs seem to have been a meeting place for all its contributors. Vuillard's entrée into this circle was most likely initiated by Thadée, whom the painter had known as early as 1884 when they were classmates at the Lycée Condorcet. Vuillard had his first one-man exhibition at the *Revue Blanche* in 1891. He contributed lithographic illustrations and covers to the review—as did his friends Toulouse-Lautrec, Bonnard, Roussel, and Vallotton. Although the scope of the journal's editorial policy extended beyond the visual arts to theater, politics, mathematics, and even bicycling, it maintained a healthy interest in the painter's world. One of its first editors, for instance, was the critic Félix Fénéon, the champion of the Neo-Impressionists; and Thadée himself devoted reviews to the art of the Impressionists or to the subject of Japanese prints (see "Icons of Inwardness").

When Misia Godebska, daughter of the Polish sculptor Cyprien Godebski, married Thadée Natanson in 1893, she brought her charm, vivacity, and prodigious musical talent to the circle of artists, poets, and journalists who contributed to the *Revue Blanche.* A pianist of extraordinary abilities, she had been a student of Gabriel Fauré; Franz Liszt had held out great hopes for her future. Although neither photographs nor paintings of Misia show her to be a great beauty, she evidently had a scintillating personality. Artists and poets of the Belle Epoque flocked to her salons. Auguste Renoir, Toulouse-Lautrec, Bonnard, and Vuillard painted portraits of Misia (fig. 81), and Mallarmé wrote a poem about her. Her friendship with Mallarmé was further strengthened when the Natansons rented a small country house at Valvins near Fontainebleau, in the immediate neighborhood of the poet's own retreat.

Vuillard's interest in Misia seems to date from the last years of the 1890s. After 1895, when Vuillard painted a series of decorative panels for Misia and Thadée, Vuillard apparently spent a great deal of time in the Natanson household. During one period he dined with the Natansons almost daily: his painting *The Luncheon* of c. 1897 (fig. 80) records a meal at Misia and Thadée's table. His journal entries for 1896 record that he spent the summer and the fall months at their house in Valvins.

Although few of the paintings of Misia are dated, almost all of them depict the salon on the rue St. Florentin near the Place de la Concorde where Misia and Thadée lived in the latter half of the 1890s. *Misia Playing the Piano,* dated 1898 (The Metropolitan Museum of Art, New York), is perhaps the earliest picture devoted to this subject. The yellow wallpaper, with its pattern of intertwined blossoms and leaves, lends a decorative note to the whole. Misia, painted in warm tones of red and yellow with a black bow at her neck, blends harmoniously into her surroundings; she constitutes a visual transition from the brightly patterned wallpaper to the austere black of the piano. Vuillard added additional warmth to the piano's solid black mass by leaving the top almost untouched by paint; the warm tawny color of the cardboard shows through in a transitional strip between the wallpaper and the piano. An oil lamp on top of the instrument is almost indistinguishable from its background.

In this tiny picture Vuillard let the pattern of the wallpaper dominate the composition, as if he intended its vivid, rich design to mirror the texture of the music flowing from Misia's hands. The arabesque curves of the pattern in the wallpaper, like the abstract, decorative lines that dominate so many of Vuillard's compositions, have been linked to the idea of music.[2]

Vuillard's works, especially his paintings of Misia, illustrate the correspondence between such design elements as the arabesque and the principle of what he called "musicality"—an "intrinsic beauty" independent of "definite emotion." In Vuillard's images of Misia in her salon, music is not physically depicted but psychologically evoked in the Symbolist manner, and all the parts of the canvas work together to create a sense of harmony.

Vuillard had written in his journal in 1894 that "There is no art without a poetic aim." By *poetic* he meant not only lyrical but also something like sublime. In the same passage he went on to propose that "There is a species of emotion particular to painting. There is an effect that results from a certain arrangement of colors, of lights, of shadows, etc. It is this that one calls the music of painting."[3] Vuillard concluded by evoking the metaphor not of poetry but of music, because to him music, of all the arts, most readily offered a sense of supreme harmony, an untraceable but undeniable effect of a certain arrangement—in this case of notes and silences. The emotion that Vuillard saw as the special province of painting was thus brought about by the musiclike orchestration of visual elements into a sense of unity that transcends the merely visual.

The association of music and painting was central to the Symbolist doctrine of synaesthesia, which rested on the principle that one sense could evoke another. Thus a color might evoke a sound or a smell, or conversely, a series of notes could bring the idea of a particular color to the mind of the listener. The relationship between the senses had been explored earlier in the century by psychophysiologists who sought to find links between the physical makeup of the sensory organs and the mind's processing of sensory data. Johann Wolfgang von Goethe, for example, felt that the five senses must share certain patterns—that there must be eight basic colors to match the notes of the octave. Although Goethe's color theory was later shaken, the desire to find psychological roots to the physiological functioning of the senses was both compelling to scientists and inspirational to poets, composers, and painters later in the century.

Charles Baudelaire, in his famous poem of 1857, "Correspondances," suggested in a few lines that there were relationships between the senses:

> Like long-held echoes, blending somewhere else
> into one deep and shadowy unison
> as limitless as darkness and as day
> the sounds, the scents, the colors correspond.
>
> There are odors succulent as young flesh
> sweet as flutes, green as any grass . . . [4]

Baudelaire's notion that "the sounds, the scents, the colors correspond" became a rallying cry for the Symbolist generation. They looked to Richard Wagner, too, whose operas were a paradigm for what he called the *Gesamtkunstwerk,* a global composition ideally embracing all the arts and sensory experiences. Among the many journals published in the 1890s, the *Revue Wagnérienne* took as its basic premise the idea of the *Gesamtkunstwerk*; the review's publisher, Theodor de Wyzewa, mixed in the circles of the Nabis, and the review was widely read among Vuillard's friends.

On the most literal level, Vuillard's paintings of Misia Natanson at the piano, or seated in proximity to her piano, may be taken as a nod toward synaesthesia. It is not so much music itself, however, as *musicality* that Vuillard seeks to evoke in these works—a mood to be conveyed less by overt reference to a musical subject than by the delicate interweaving of color and line, the harmony and melody of painting.

These lush, highly patterned paintings strike the viewer as works created for a specific decorative function, although they were, in fact, easel paintings and not decorative panels. The concept of "the decorative," however, is one of the central tenets of Symbolism, and it is in these works more than any others that Vuillard achieved the synthesis that Albert Aurier prescribed. According to Aurier's strictures, a Symbolist painting should be:

1. *Ideist,* for its unique ideal will be the expression of the Idea.

2. *Symbolist,* for it will express this Idea by means of forms.

3. *Synthetist,* for it will present these forms, these signs, according to a method which is generally understandable.

4. *Subjective,* for the object will never be considered as an object, but as a sign of an idea perceived by the subject.

5. [It is consequently] *Decorative*—for decorative painting, in its proper sense, as the Egyptians and, very probably the Greeks and the Primitives understood it, is nothing other than a manifestation of art at once subjective, synthetic, symbolist and ideist. [5]

80 ❧

The Luncheon

c. 1897

oil on canvas, 15¼ x 13¹³⁄₁₆ inches, Yale

University Art Gallery, New Haven,

Connecticut; the Katharine Ordway

Collection

81 ❧

Portrait of Misia

c. 1897

oil on cardboard mounted on canvas, 21 x

19⅜ inches, private collection, Mexico

City

Vuillard's art, as a whole, responded to the notion of the "decorative" as defined by Aurier: a harmonious arrangement of color and lines which in and of themselves had a moral completeness apart from what they depicted. But the decorative also came to mean the move away from easel painting to an art that embraced the architecture of the wall.

Taking as an inspiration Puvis de Chavannes's noble compositions, which in their grand scale did not pierce the flatness of the wall of illusionistic perspective, Vuillard and the other Nabis readily took on commissions to paint panels for entire rooms. These decorative panels are of great interest, but Vuillard's exploration of the decorative in Aurier's terms is not limited to works created for a purely decorative function. All of Vuillard's works of the 1890s partake of the decorative aesthetic in their sumptuous arrangement of line and color and the layering of pattern and arabesque. His paintings of Misia Natanson dating from the end of the decade, however, realize dual Symbolist goals: the decorative arrangement of forms and the evocation of a synaesthetic union of the senses.

The year 1898, the same year in which Vuillard immersed himself in paintings of Misia and her husband, marked a turning point for the Natanson fortunes and consequently for the couple's relationship. In that year, the review mounted a spirited defense of Alfred Dreyfus, a Jewish officer who had been convicted unjustly of treason. As a result of the politicization of the publication, its character became radically changed, its contributors eventually moved on to other endeavors, and it began a slow but noticeable decline. The waning fortunes of the review inevitably exerted pressure on Thadée Natanson and apparently affected his relationship with his wife. It is probable, in fact, that Thadée encouraged a flirtation between Misia and a potential benefactor of the *Revue Blanche,* Alfred Edwards. By 1903, when the review ceased publication, the Natansons were at an impasse. In 1904 they divorced, and the next year Misia married Edwards.

In the painting *Misia and Thadée Natanson* (fig. 79), the piano, although it sits unplayed, is nonetheless the largest element of the composition. Misia sits back in her chair with her eyes closed. As in other paintings of the same subject, she blends with her surroundings but is not overwhelmed by them in the way that Marie Vuillard is eclipsed in the dining paintings. The yellow wallpaper, repeated in the upholstery of the chair in which she is sitting, creates a golden halo around her. This tone is carried through to the dress she wears and even to the color of her hair. Vuillard gave Misia the entire foreground space. Visually linked to the ebony piano by the black bow of her dress, she seems to be embraced by the tapestry or shawl that covers the piano, stretching like a horizontal band across the canvas.

Even when men are present, Misia dominates the paintings of her salon; here Thadée is pushed to the top right corner of the canvas, trapped between the piano and the wall. Vuillard used the shawl-covered piano to separate Misia and Thadée physically and to indicate the emotional distance between them. The upper half of the canvas is dominated by two strong horizontals: the wallpaper and the tapestry (or shawl). That the latter is actually covering the piano is made evident only by the indication of the instrument's legs and keyboard that appear at the extreme left of the painting. The small vase of flowers placed on the piano at the edge of the shawl paraliels Thadée's figure at the canvas's right margin. Although the viewer reads the shawl as a horizontal division of the painting, Vuillard in fact has obscured its details on the right-hand side. Thus, while the left side of the canvas portrays in naturalistic detail many objects in the room, such as the painting on the wall, the vase of flowers, and the stack of music next to the piano, the right side remains shadowy. Misia faces left toward an unseen source of light, and everything behind her, including her husband, is obscure. Vuillard's portrayals of Misia are orchestrated so that all elements play a supporting role to her.

When Vuillard discussed the musicality of his paintings, he referred to the proper relationship between lines, shapes, and colors on the canvas. The layering of pattern and the close tonal range in the palette of this painting recall Vuillard's interest in medieval tapestries with their tightly knit compositions and their intricately detailed designs. Tapestry, like music, seems to have served Vuillard as a metaphor for the decorative form he sought in painting. After a trip to see the Cluny tapestries in 1894, when he was painting the decorative panels *Jardins Publics* for Alexandre Natanson, he wrote about the inspiration he had received from these works.

> Visited Cluny yesterday. Tapestries and missal illuminations. Calendars. In the tapestries I think that in enlarging pure and simple my little panel that'll make the subject of a decoration. The humble subjects of these decorations at Cluny! Expression of an *intimate feeling* on a bigger surface that's all. The same thing as a Chardin, for example . . . A little morsel, very old, in flat, common tints, the very powerful charm of color, glaring colors on a light ground . . . There are two occupations in me: the study of exterior perception, filled with painful experiences, dangerous for my humor and my nerves. And the study of pictorial decoration rarely possible besides much more limited, but which ought to give me the tranquility of a worker—think back often to the Cluny tapestries.[6]

The buildup of pattern in the paintings of Misia, even the floral motif of the background wallpaper and the layering of patterned rugs on the floor, recall the compounded images of the Cluny tapestries. Moreover, in such works as the *Interior with Three Lamps* (see fig. 90) or *Misia and Thadée Natanson* (fig. 82), a tapestry actually hangs behind the piano in the salon of the rue St. Florentin apartment, becoming in the latter work the flat, decorative ground against which Vuillard places the protagonists of his picture.[7]

"Pictorial decoration," however, was not Vuillard's sole occupation. He says that he has two occupations, one pictorial decoration, the other "the study of exterior perception," a study that he finds fraught with pain, even dangerous. Thus the drama of the subject, as well as its decorative qualities, is important to Vuillard's paintings of the Natansons. In focusing on Misia and relegating Thadée to the background,

109

82 &

Misia and Thadée Natanson

c. 1898

oil on cardboard, 19 x 20¼ inches,

private foundation, California

Vuillard made *Misia and Thadée Natanson* (see fig. 79) a statement about a relationship with which he had been intimately involved for some time. In this painting of Misia, more than in any other, Vuillard depicts his private relationship with her, in which the two of them share a space that excludes Thadée (who is nonetheless present). And yet Misia too was in some way closed to Vuillard: her eyes are shut in the painting and she is in her own world.[8]

Vuillard seems to have grown quite close to the couple in about 1896, when he spent several months at their country home at Valvins. On Christmas Eve 1896, he wrote in his journal: "Thadée and his wife [a] very good time. Tenderness, desires of work, ambitions and sensualities . . . home at 4 in the morning, slept until noon. uncertainty and conflicting desires. An abundance of memories."[9]

It seems clear from the paintings that Vuillard was entranced by, if not infatuated with, Misia. She recounted in her autobiography a vignette about Vuillard's silent declaration of love for her. While they were walking in the woods one day, probably in 1897, Misia tripped: Vuillard grabbed her, looked deep into her eyes, and burst into sobs. Because Misia's autobiography is not wholly reliable, we can only guess from how Vuillard painted Misia what he actually felt for her. It is true, however, that his series of pictures devoted to Misia are among his most sensual and strikingly beautiful and that when Thadée is present in them, he is almost always overlooked.

Several photographs of Misia and Thadée taken by Vuillard offer an instructive comparison to his paintings of them. It is likely that Vuillard began experimenting with making photographs, using an ordinary Kodak camera, sometime around 1895. After 1907, when he began recording daily entries in his journal, Vuillard made constant, almost daily references to photography; several hundred photographs remain in his family's possession. A journal entry—"afterwards in the studio [I] worked with a photo and a pastel from summer"—leads one to believe that, at least in the early twentieth century, Vuillard did use his photographs as aides-mémoires for his paintings.[10] The relationship between Vuillard's paintings and his photographs, however, is far more complex, the subtle deformations of the photographic space often bear a striking resemblance to Vuillard's painted compositions. Because of slow shutter speeds, Vuillard's photographs of his interiors had to be as carefully composed as his paintings. Like his paintings, these photographs reveal Vuillard's highly personal aesthetic.[11]

Although instantaneous photography was possible by the late 1880s, Vuillard, like Degas before him, resorted to an older, more formal, and more difficult use of the medium.[12] Vuillard's photographic experiments also followed Degas's path away from what Eugenia Janis has called the "indiscriminate tendencies of instantaneity" toward a "photographic theater" of family and friends.[13] Degas had deliberately made the process of picture-taking as difficult as possible, closing curtains and lighting lamps, forcing his sitters to pose for long, slow exposures. His gloomy images often do not describe his subjects in detail, instead relying on a Mallarméan atmosphere of suggestion.[14]

83

Photograph by Vuillard of Misia and

Thadée Natanson, 1898. Paris,

Bibliothèque Nationale

Although gross deformations of perspective were usually avoided in late nineteenth-century photography, there were nonetheless persistent oddities within the photographed space: planes of depth were elided, elements in the foreground of the composition became exaggeratedly enlarged, and background elements shrank correspondingly.[15] Vuillard possibly welcomed such distortions in his photographs, as they resulted in a manipulation of space similar to the kind of manipulation he had employed in his paintings since the early 1890s.

In a photograph of Misia and Thadée from 1898 (fig. 83) Vuillard manipulated the forms and composition in ways that he would continue to explore in both photography and painting for the next decade. The photograph shows Thadée, looming in the foreground, slightly out of focus because of his proximity to the lens, while in the distance Misia sits in a chair against the back wall. Thadée's solid bulk is emphasized by the broad expanse of his suit and further reinforced by the dark door in the background that frames his head. A potted tree curving in the upper right corner echoes the shape of his head. Misia, on the other hand, is surrounded by the distracting paraphernalia of the room—the piano, with a cloth, a lamp, and several vases on top, a mirror hanging on the wall, a rocking chair, and a painting on the patterned wallpaper—all easily recognizable as belonging to Misia's salon on the rue St. Florentin. Although much smaller than Thadée in the photograph, Misia is literally its focal point. Thadée forms a weighty curve from upper right to lower left across which the viewer focuses on the clearer image of Misia.

A contemporary photograph by Vuillard of this same couple at their country house (fig. 84) reveals that he consistently focused on Misia even though Thadée's bulky frame was in the foreground. Here, however, the meaning is very clear. With his back to the camera, Thadée leans with his elbows on the dining room table; behind him, her chair pushed away from the table, Misia looks directly at Vuillard. Where a dark painting in the previous photograph had isolated her head against the busy wallpaper, here she is virtually crowned by a potted plant, whose palm leaves appear to spring from her head. Other elements of the photograph reveal the care with which Vuillard arranged the scene to maintain Misia's centrality in the composition: the diagonal created by the two foreground chairs leads the eye in a direct line to her torso. The chair backs and slats form orthogonals that suggest a strong recession into depth, tempered by the horizontal lines of the mantelpiece and the cupboard divider. The shape formed by Misia's shoulders, neck, and head against the wall provides a vertical thrust between these two architecturally strong horizontals. Because Thadée's shoulders continue on the line of the mantel and because his jacket, like the architectural elements, is light in color, Misia's dark form is all the more noticeable.

The clear indication of recession in the photograph of Misia and Thadée in the dining room was nullified in the salon photograph. By condensing the figures and objects so that one plane laps against another, by amplifying Thadée's bulk in the foreground while diminishing Misia in the background, and by eliminating the space

84

Left: Photograph by Vuillard of Misia and

Thadée Natanson at their country house,

"Le Relais," at Villeneuve, c. 1899.

Archives Antoine Salomon, Paris

85

Right: Photograph by Vuillard of the

Natanson country house with Romain

Coolus, c. 1899. Archives Antoine Salo-

mon, Paris

between them, Vuillard effectively flattened the image's pictorial space. Curiously enough, the situation of the figures is reversed in the painting *Misia and Thadée Natanson* (see fig. 79), where she is pointedly large compared to Thadée's receding form. Both the painting and the photographs exhibit radical shifts in scale that are characteristic distortions of the photographic lens. Because Vuillard consistently exploits this distortion in both mediums, it appears to have been a conscious artistic choice rather than a mere consequence of a primitive technology.

It should be noted, however, that a perceptual phenomenon understood since the Renaissance also creates the same spatial distortion. When the spectator stands close to the subject, the angle of vision becomes wide and thus exaggerates the foreground while abruptly diminishing objects in the background.[16] This phenomenon is actually created only by constructing a representation of correct perspective from a close viewpoint. It is rarely experienced so pointedly in nature because people tend to move their eyes when they are uncomfortably close to an object. In the generation before Vuillard, Impressionist painters such as Degas and Gustave Caillebotte had exploited this scientifically determined perspective without the immediate aid of the camera, inspired, perhaps, by the spatial distortions they observed in Japanese prints. Vuillard's manipulations, combining perspectival constructions with distortions learned from photography, represent an individual approach to composition.

The camera imposes certain limitations on the artist. In order to focus directly on Misia in the photograph of her in her dining room, Vuillard placed her at the center of the composition and at the lens's focal point, leaving the other objects in the lens's field of vision slightly blurred. In painting the artist can control the deformities

113

of light and space and can focus to suit his purpose. In his painting of Misia sitting rapt in front of the piano, Vuillard bathed his primary subject in a full light and depicted legibly only those elements of the room that she faces. Everything else—where her husband stands behind her and to the right—is obscured either by scumbled paint strokes, by muddy color, or by the scratching out of specific areas of the painting, such as the features of Thadée's face. To emphasize Misia's centrality in the painting, he depicted only her torso and her head clearly, leaving the long skirt of her dress blurred and in shadow. Because the yellow material of her skirt takes up a considerable amount of space, to have painted it with any greater precision would have distracted from Misia herself. Vuillard seemed to zero in on the black bow of Misia's dress as if to reinforce the power of her central, iconic pose.

Photographs can provide other kinds of information about paintings: not only what the paintings represent but also where they actually hung in a room or how they related to other objects in that room. In another photograph of the Natanson country house from about 1899 (fig. 85), Romain Coolus sits at a desk beside a fireplace. The fireplace resembles the one featured in the photograph of Misia and Thadée in the dining room, having a simple mantelpiece with a pedimented overmantel flanked by two Doric piers. A painting is framed in a molding above another molding inset with a mirror. In the photograph of Misia and Thadée, a landscape hangs in the upper section of the mantel, but in this photograph a painting by Vuillard hangs there.

The painting, *Mother and Child* from about 1899 (fig. 86), depicts the living room on the rue St. Florentin. Misia is shown sitting on a chaise longue, holding up her niece, Mimi Godebska. The patterning in this picture is especially dense and complex: not only do the walls and chaise have different and distinctive coverings, but the screen that separates them also has a different pattern in every section. The chaise, which projects toward the viewer, stretching from the background into the extreme foreground where its front leg is cropped by the bottom of the canvas, defies the laws of perspective: while its back appears to be parallel to the back wall, the front is tipped in the direction of the viewer. The picture's eventual placement above the fireplace might have determined this distorted rendering, which actually might have been correct from the vantage point of the viewer below. Still other inconsistencies may be noted: the back wall appears to be flat, but the picture hanging to the right of the screen is clearly on a side wall, indicating that we are in fact looking at a corner—the two walls join where the two right sections of the screen come together.

Although the background wallpaper is dominated by yellow tones, which Vuillard has picked up in the left section of the screen, the entire composition revolves around the golden glow of the box or chest upon which the baby is perched. This intense yellow could have created an imbalance in the composition, but Vuillard surrounded the object with the rich blue of Misia's dress and the red of the drapery on the right. The three primary colors are balanced by the putty tone of the mantelpiece on the extreme right. The careful balance of color is matched by the sinuously flowing

lines in the frame of the screen, which cuts across the composition and is continued by the line of the picture frame on the wall, and in the patterns of each object. The composition's harmony comes from its completeness and its resolution. It is decorative in the grand sense in which Aurier used the word but also in terms of its intended placement in a specific interior. The picture must be seen in terms of the environment for which it was intended—set off in the severe molding of the overmantel, surrounded by patterned wallpaper, mirror reflection and all.

The Nabis' interest in decoration has often been discussed in terms of their embrace of large decorative environments and their abandonment of the easel picture. As Dom Verkade, a fellow Nabi, wrote later:

> Toward the beginning of 1890, a war cry went up from one studio to another: No more easel painting! . . . The wall should remain a surface, should not be pierced for the representation of infinite horizons. There are not paintings, there are only decorations.[17]

Vuillard's many commissions to execute decorations in the 1890s are abundant evidence of his belief in the validity of the mural surface, but the obviously "decorative" qualities of these works have overshadowed similar qualities in the easel paintings that the artist continued to produce throughout the decade. Vuillard's continuing

86

Mother and Child

1899

oil on cardboard, 20 x 23 inches, Glasgow

Art Gallery and Museum, Scotland

87 ❧

Woman in a Striped Dress

c. 1895

oil on canvas, 25⅞ x 23⅛ inches,

National Gallery of Art, Washington,

D.C.; collection of Mr. and Mrs. Paul

Mellon

88

The Salon,

rue Saint-Florentin

1897

oil on paper on wood, 17⅞ x 20¼ inches,

Foundation E. G. Bührle Collection,

Zürich

struggle to flatten the picture space, to eschew the "representation of infinite horizons," and his preference for the "flat, common tints" associated with mural decorations are indicative of the degree to which "decorative" elements found a role in his more conventionally scaled paintings.

It is difficult to establish with certainty whether *Mother and Child* hung in the room shown in the photograph of Thadée and Misia (see fig. 84). The fireplaces appear a bit different, the wallpaper is not the same, and the toiletries on the mantel in the second photograph indicate a more private setting. The subjects of the paintings in the overmantels may reflect the nature of the rooms; a landscape hangs in the dining room and the image of maternity, although it represents a reception room, hangs in a more private area of the apartment.

The only painting to show with clarity the location of the chaise and screen in relation to the rest of the room is *The Salon, rue Saint-Florentin* (fig. 88). The chaise is shown here in the lower left corner, backed by the screen and a palm. In this picture Vuillard has painted the entire scene out of focus, save the image in the glass over the fireplace that reflects the wall over the piano on the opposite side of the room. In the mirror a horizontal red strip presents a reverse image of a painting called *The Album (The Conversation)* (Mr. and Mrs. Walter Annenberg, Rancho Mirage, California), one of five decorative panels Vuillard painted for Thadée and Misia in 1895. The five panels, which are now dispersed, represent one of Vuillard's most beautiful decorative series. Unlike most of his other large ensembles which depicted scenes out of doors, these panels, painted almost entirely in warm reds, oranges, and yellows, gloried in the aspects of quotidian life that normally were reserved for the small easel paintings. Although it is certain that they were painted as a decorative group, they are remarkably varied in scale and in composition. *The Album* is an exaggerated horizontal, while *Embroiderers Near a Window* (The Museum of Modern Art, New York) is pronouncedly vertical. *Woman in a Striped Dress* (fig. 87), another painting from the series, is much smaller than the others. It is not yet clear, furthermore, how the Natansons employed the paintings in their interiors.

The Album figures again in the background of *Misia at the Piano with Her Brother Cipa Godebski* (fig. 89), where Misia appears seated at the piano, and her brother Cipa stands beside a doorway behind her and to the left. In front of the piano a sewing table holds a tea service with several cups. The brightest object in the room is the tall lamp on top of the piano. A focal element in many of Vuillard's compositions of women sewing and the family dining, the lamp in this painting takes on a different role. Although lit, it casts neither direct nor dramatic light; instead, Vuillard played with its placement in the picture to make it appear to be part of the painting against the wall. The thin columnar base of the lamp blends into the background wallpaper, and the curvilinear forms of its bowl and glass blend with the patterns and colors of the painting.

In the painting's context, Misia herself becomes a three-dimensional extension of this patterning, carrying the red hues of the decorative panel on the wall into the

117

space of the picture. Vuillard portrayed her with a shirt of brighter orange-red than that of the painting on the wall. This combination, coupled with her auburn hair, creates a concentrated group of red tones in the center of the composition. Although he painted Misia's face very solidly, with small, densely layered, parallel strokes, Vuillard violently scratched her red shirt with the wooden end of his brush handle, adding a frenzy to the otherwise tranquil image of contemplative music-making.[18]

The eye moves out from the reds in the middle of the composition to the yellows that flank it, traveling across the picture from one area of yellow to another. While the left side of the composition appears to depict a set of glass doors with a yellow half curtain, we know from other paintings of this scene that a hallway or vestibule separated this area from the salon. The solid yellow of the curtains picks up similar tones in the door jamb, in the wallpaper, in the lamp and in the yellow flowers in the painting on the wall, and in the golden glow on the tea table. All the architectural elements are bathed in golden light.

The transitional element in the composition is the figure of Cipa, who hovers between the two rooms and is depicted almost entirely in shadow, except for a greenish light on his cheek and forehead. A massive form in unmodulated brown paint, he almost appears part of the furniture of the room, not at all the foreboding presence his looming figure might have introduced. It is as if Vuillard wanted to focus on the music rising from Misia's inspired playing, and thus he showered her with pattern, color, and light. Her diminished size in the composition indicates that even she becomes small compared to the power of her music.

Le Pot de grès, another panel from the Natanson decorations, hangs in the background of a painting of Misia with her husband and the painter Félix Vallotton (*Misia and Vallotton in the Dining Room, rue Saint-Florentin,* fig. 92). This portrait, dated 1899, makes it possible to date the other two canvases featuring the same decorative panels to about the same time. Misia is seen in profile looking out of the picture to the right and dipping into a bowl of coffee or chocolate, possibly to feed her dog that can be seen at the bottom of the canvas with its paw on Misia's lap. Vallotton stands directly behind Misia but faces left. He appears to be in conversation with Thadée, who is barely indicated at the extreme left of the composition; his portly frame and his pipe identify him conclusively, but once again Vuillard has reduced Thadée almost to a nonpresence. The physical elements of this carefully contrived composition are tightly knit: Misia's yellow scarf connects her visually to the wallpaper; Vallotton's solid blue jacket frames Misia's body and separates her from the surrounding pattern; Vallotton's head is framed by the decorative panel on the wall; and the vase of flowers in the painting on the wall is visually echoed by the small vase on the sideboard below. What is most telling about this painting, however, is the total lack of psychological connection among its characters. The two figures who are clearly visible look in opposite directions, and a conversation takes place between one figure who is visible and another who can barely be discerned.

Throughout the paintings of Misia, Vuillard plays on what he had called the

89

Misia at the Piano with Her Brother Cipa Godebski

1897

oil on cardboard, 24 x 20⅛ inches,

Kunsthalle Karlsruhe, West Germany

90 ❧

Interior with Three Lamps, rue Saint-Florentin

1898

Overleaf: oil on canvas, 22⅞ x 37 inches,

Gustav Zumsteg, Zürich

91 ❧

Interior with Three People

1899

oil on wood, 18⅛ x 10¼ inches, private

collection, Zürich

92 ❧

Misia and Vallotton in the

Dining Room, rue Saint-

Florentin

1899

oil on cardboard, 28⅜ x 20 1/16 inches,

William Kelly Simpson

"decorative qualities" of objects. Thus elements of *interior decoration* become used for *decorative* ends. But Vuillard is also concerned with the psychological or emotional associations of objects in these works. Because they constitute an unusually coherent ensemble, these paintings, more than any others, make clear how objects can have meaning beyond their "pure and simple" shapes. Vuillard often used the shapes of furniture to express something about the people he depicted. As the round dinner table, for example, becomes an objective symbol of the family's psychological alienation, so, too, the salon on the rue St. Florentin, with the piano as its focal point, provides a setting expressive of the characters of Misia and her husband Thadée.

122

Vuillard's depictions of Misia and Thadée Natanson's apartment celebrate the sumptuous color and the lusciousness of the decor in general. The most distinguishing feature of these paintings of Misia, which indeed serves to identify them as a cohesive group, is the paper that covers the walls of the salon. The wallpaper, seen in the photographs and the paintings, is composed of an undulating, crisscrossed pattern of dark green leaves and yellow flowers. With its tenuous balance between naturalism and formalism, the design of the fabric and wallpaper resembles those designed by members of the English arts and crafts movement. Although it is similar to William Morris's chrysanthemum pattern, it is probably a French adaptation of Morris's work.[19]

The wallpaper forms the backdrop for each of the paintings of Misia. In the painting of Misia and Thadée, not only are the walls hung with this paper, but the late Louis XV chair Misia is seated upon is upholstered in a fabric of the same pattern. Vuillard varies his treatment of the pattern from picture to picture. Sometimes, as in the painting of *Misia Playing the Piano* (The Metropolitan Museum of Art, New York) or in *Interior with Three People* (fig. 91), he emphasizes the geometry

of the repeat in the pattern, leaving an impression of a diagonal grid. In other works, such as the portrait of *Misia and Vallotton* (see fig. 92), he asserts its flat floral motif. In still others, such as *Misia and Thadée Natanson* (see fig. 79) or *Misia at the Piano with Her Brother Cipa Godebski* (see fig. 89), the pattern takes on a shimmering, almost glowing quality, enhancing the moody atmosphere that pervades the paintings.

The furniture and objects in Misia's salon are similarly employed to convey subtle shades of meaning. The salon on the rue St. Florentin can be seen best in *Interior with Three Lamps, rue Saint-Florentin* (fig. 90), dated 1899. Here the golden lamps are scattered about the room, on the piano, and on the tables at either side. The familiar yellow wallpaper and the piano covered with a shawl identify the room, but the central object is the bentwood rocking chair on which the Natansons' friend Romain Coolus is sitting. This rocker, also visible in the photograph of Misia and Thadée in their salon and in other paintings by Vuillard from the turn of the century, is of the type made by the Thonet manufactory, which since mid-century had perfected the technique of bending wood into elegantly curved shapes. By the 1890s Thonet chairs took a prominent role in Vuillard's paintings, because their rococo curves lent a sinuous, linear arabesque to the compositions, in this case creating a paisley shape at the center of his painting. In Misia's salon, the rocking chair, like the

95

La Table au grand abat-jour

1897–98

lithograph, 5½ x 8¼ inches, as

reproduced in Roger-Marx, L'Oeuvre gravé

de Vuillard, no. 12

chaise longue on which she reclines in *The Red Peignoir* (fig. 93), becomes an emblem of feminine sensuality—a bentwood odalisque—part of the feminine environment that was so dominated by Misia's personality.

Vuillard also uses the lamps in this room—glowing through their ruffled silk or glass shades—to illuminate, and at times to obscure, the figures in the compositions. In the *Interior with Three People* (see fig. 91), as in the *Interior with Three Lamps* (see fig. 90), the golden light of the oil lamps acts as an emblem of the camaraderie present in the room, a symbol of enlightenment or inspiration. Likewise, a lamp is the dominant element in the painting *The Card Game* (fig. 94), and a related lithograph (fig. 95). In the lithograph the composition is almost entirely devoted to the lampshade, which dominates the top portion of the page and blocks the heads of a number of figures. On the left, Alfred Natanson sits in profile; his wife, Marthe Mellot, sits on the other side next to Thadée, whose profile complements his brother's.[20] The two brothers, with similar features and beards, form a decorative inner frame to the composition as Vuillard portrays little besides the outlines of their features, and they constitute the transition from blank paper to the scene itself. Although the composition has previously been described with five figures, one can barely discern at least six and possibly seven people in the composition.[21] The liveliness of the dinner conversation is conveyed by the busy lines that connect the figures—the whimsical outline of the hair of the woman in the lower left connects to Alfred Natanson's arm; his beard in turn touches the shoulder of the woman next to him, whose forehead touches the edge of the lampshade. This line sweeps over to what may be the outline of a figure and then touches the sleeve of Marthe Mellot, whose other shoulder connects to Thadée's nose. Although the overwhelming presence of the lampshade flattens the composition, the exaggerated difference in size between the two brothers, who extend from the top to the bottom of the composition, and the women sitting next to them serves to indicate a great depth and to represent a viewpoint extremely close to the picture plane. Vuillard's manipulations cause the pictorial space in this work to hover between flatness and depth. Although the lamp dominates the center of the composition, it casts no dramatic shadows. All the faces around the table are clearly and evenly illuminated.

Vuillard used a similar composition to depict the same group of people in *The Card Game* (see fig. 94). Lampshades create light backdrops for the profiles of the Natanson brothers, who flank the sides of the composition in much the same way as in the lithograph. In the painting Vuillard does away with the paraphernalia of the table, so the eerie lamp light, exactly at the level of the four figures' heads, helps to focus the viewer's attention on the faces. The only other area of the picture Vuillard highlights is Misia Natanson's hands—clearly it is she who holds the trump.

CONCLUSION

*E*douard Vuillard's interiors of the 1890s, so private and so subjective, begin to reveal themselves as the viewer moves from canvas to canvas, gradually arriving at a deeply felt knowledge of the painter's inner world. We come to recognize familiar pieces of furniture, patterns of wallpaper, the sumptuous textiles and carpets, and salient gestures as well as characteristic silhouettes of Vuillard's family and closest friends. The intimacy we develop with the works of art is not only familial and psychological but also physical: the consistently small scale of the paintings requires that we examine them, one by one, at close range.

The disturbing aspects of Vuillard's canvases, those distortions in the pictorial space that create an uneasy sense of airlessness, are emphasized by their small size. This phenomenon was discussed by Hermann Ludwig von Helmholtz, a prominent psychophysiologist of the mid-nineteenth century.[1] He theorized that a viewer tends to look at a small painting from up close, thereby creating a wide angle of vision between the two eyes and the canvas. A large painting, viewed from far away, may produce a retinal image of the same size, but the angle of vision is narrower because the eyes converge on an object that is farther away. He concluded that small paintings can create a disturbing effect because the eyes must converge at a more extreme angle.

In choosing to paint these interiors on a small scale, Vuillard ensured that the viewer would examine the surface—not only the image—of his art; facture becomes an integral part of the meaning of the work. The contrast between Vuillard's glossy and matte colors, for example, is most readily apparent when the pictures are seen close at hand. The telling differences in brush stroke that distinguish areas of a torso or different pieces of material can only be appreciated when the pictures are viewed so closely as to obliterate the world outside the picture frame. Thus in a picture such as *The Dressmakers* (see fig. 8), what appears at first to be a composition made entirely of flat planes of solid colors is in fact an active ensemble of complex brush strokes, each catching the light in a different way.

Perhaps the most striking aspect of Vuillard's facture is what he chose *not* to paint in his canvases. The areas of the canvas or the cardboard that Vuillard left blank play as important a role in his compositions as do the pigmented areas. From pictures painted as early as 1891, such as *The Seamstress* (see fig. 11), to others finished late in his career, we can see how Vuillard exploited the potential of the nonpainted areas. The area in *The Seamstress* that Vuillard chose to leave untouched is central to the composition, taking on a bow shape all its own. Vuillard was aware of the power of this shape: in an early sketch, he also left blank the same section of the woman's torso. In other paintings, such as *L'Atelier* (see fig. 28), Vuillard rendered the foreground figure's ambiguous position in space by making her dress out of dark dots on top of raw cardboard. Thus, although we see her as part of the foreground, she merges with the background as well, making her exact position unclear.

In some self-portraits, Vuillard chose to leave the eyes blank. The eyes must connect with the viewer in a self-portrait: in any other kind of portrait the subject can look away, but in a self-portrait the subject is the artist regarding himself. By leaving the eyes blank in a canvas of brightly colored, solid forms, Vuillard has focused the viewer's attention on the very part of the picture that is essential for connection, creating a disequilibrium. So while the unpainted areas of the canvas play a crucial spatial role—merging foreground and background, distinguishing forms, or creating a sense of atmosphere—the choice of what to leave untouched is by no means random.

It has been said that the complex spatial role of Vuillard's dots and patterns may have inspired Picasso in his Synthetic Cubist images of 1914, where dots float over the surface of the canvas and provide a point of reference behind and around which other shapes float.[2] But even before this, Picasso and Braque could have taken their cue for their experiments in collage from Vuillard's areas of unpainted canvas. The ambiguities of space and meaning that are inspired by Vuillard's blank sections of canvas are exactly the kinds of visual complexities explored by the Cubist masters in their collages, in which the raw paper takes on several roles at once—spatial, atmospheric, and physical.

Vuillard's art of the 1890s, radical in its own time, was an inspiration for experimental painting of the early twentieth century. And yet, ironically, his own art took a more conservative path at the same time that a new generation of painters was pushing the ideas of representation and abstraction to further limits. Vuillard, whose early inspiration was the old masters of the Louvre, dedicated the last forty years of his career to becoming the modern heir to what he saw as the great French tradition.

Eustache Le Sueur, Nicolas Poussin, and above all Eugène Delacroix, whose journals he would quote almost daily in later years, became his models. As his subjects began to come from the outside world instead of from the insular, psychically charged world of family and friends, his art turned more to tradition than to hermetic self-absorption. Vuillard's pictures from the twentieth century, mostly commissioned portraits, are of interest for their high-key color combinations, among other things. But out of step with the tenets of picture-making posited by a new generation, Vuillard never again shared with us his innermost thoughts about himself or his art.

NOTES

Vuillard's journal entries cited here in the Notes section were translated in the text by George T.M. Shackelford.

The first volume of the journal, comprising two separate notebooks, will be cited here as EV I.1 [journal I, carnet 1] and EV I.2 [journal I, carnet 2], followed by a page reference (the letter "v" used here indicates that the information cited is on the verso of the numbered page). When possible, a date for the entry is given. For further information, see note 2 of "Beyond the Mirror."

Introduction

1. . . . la façon dont les formes se détachent les unes des autres a cette idée le rapport de lumière et par conséquent de couleur, de forme aussi (espace occupé) dans lequel une forme est avec ce qui l'environne; se distingue vaudrait mieux que détacher, qui implique l'idée d'éloignement cette idée d'éloignement est une idée non une sensation première qui tient je crois avoir vu une explication indiquée: les yeux étant deux et à une certaine distance l'un de l'autre. Et bien ce sentiment, la connaissance de ce rapport est la Verité qu'il faut avoir et que l'on écrira sur la toile ou sur le papier. Sans quoi si l'on n'a pas de modèle, de sujet, on fait l'oeuvre d'un insecte se promenant sur du papier avec de l'encre au doigt. A quoi bon toute cette écriture? Si En relevant les yeux sur une peinture ou la nature je *veux* observer, je tombe dans le faux. On observe, on ne peut vouloir observer. L'émotion contenue (l'observation) peut seule donner est la première condition d'une oeuvre d'art, avant l'esprit de méthode et l'intelligence pratique qui naissent de l'âme même qui subit cette émotion.
EV I.2, 32v–33 (2 April 1891)

Beyond the Mirror: The Self-portraits

. . . concevoir bien un tableau comme un ensemble d'accords.
EV I.2 p. 71v (31 August 1890)

1. At the Lycée Condorcet, Vuillard met Thadée and Alexandre Natanson, Maurice Denis, and Ker-Xavier Roussel. Denis and Roussel were a year behind him, but Thadée was in the same class. Others who attended the Lycée Condorcet and who entered Vuillard's circle either directly or indirectly were Henri Bergson, Jacques-Emile Blanche, Romain Coolus, Aurélien-Marie Lugné-Poë, Marcel Proust, Jules Romains, and Jean Cocteau.

Archives at the Lycée Condorcet reveal that in *Rhétorique,* the penultimate year of *lycée,* Vuillard was the outstanding mathematics student in his class. This might have encouraged him to enter *Mathématiques élémentaires* in his last year instead of *Philosophie,* which was the normal course of study.

The second chapter of my unpublished doctoral thesis examines in depth the roots of Vuillard's aesthetic in his *lycée* education. The best source for an account of Symbolist roots in the *lycée* is Filiz Eda Burhan's "Vision and Visionaries: Nineteenth Century Psychological Theory, the Occult Sciences and the Formation of the Symbolist Aesthetic in France," Ph.D. dissertation, Princeton University, 1979.

2. All the journals are housed in the Institut de France under catalogue numbers ms. 5396–99. The more than fifty volumes cover the entire span of Vuillard's life; the last entry was for 2 June 1940, less than three weeks before he died. The Institut listing is as follows, but does not include a supplementary donation of volumes which cover the years from 1926 to 1929:

> Volume I (Inv. no. 5396), *Crouqis et esquisses au crayon et à la plume; notes:*
> part 1. 1890 (this is incorrect; the volume actually covers the years 1888–1890).
> part 2. 1890–1905.
>
> Volumes II-IV *Journal:*
> Vol. II (Inv. no. 5397) 1907–1916: 9 carnets.
> Vol. III (Inv. no. 5398) 1916–1922: 11 carnets.
> Vol. IV (Inv. no. 5399) 1929–1940: 13 carnets.

The journals are regular composition books with lined paper, and measure 220 × 170 mm and 150 × 90.5 mm. They were given to the Institut in 1943 by Ker-Xavier Roussel and his wife Marie, Vuillard's sister.

Both of the first two volumes were purchased at E. Normand, 32 and 34, rue du Havre, next door to the Lycée Condorcet where Vuillard went to school until 1886.

Volume I is numbered from pp. 1–65, and for the most part the pages are written consecutively and right side up. The first volume is notable for the preponderance of sketches. The second, consisting of 91 pages, contains several loose sheets of paper, and while heavily illustrated, dedicates more space to Vuillard's prose. It is important to note the number of pages given to each year in the second volume, so the reader will be aware of why the citations fall into given blocks of time: 1890: pp. 1–25v (26 novembre); 1891: pp. 30 (mars)-37; 1894: pp. 41v (10 juillet)-55 (8 novembre); 1895: pp. 55v (19 mars)-57v (30 octobre); 1896: p. 57v; 1897: p. 57v; 1898: p. 57v; 1905: p. 58. After this, randomly inserted pages cover the same period of time but focus mostly on the years 1890, 1891, and 1894.

Vuillard's daily entries, which continue until his death, begin only in 1907, so the important decade between 1896 and 1906 is virtually unaccounted for. While these journals do not rank with Delacroix's, whose poetic thoughts Vuillard often cited in later years, they nonetheless offer an intimate and insightful view into daily life at the turn of the century. The reader witnesses a crucial change in the artist/author from a young idealist at the end of the nineteenth century to a somewhat bourgeois boulevardier at the beginning of the twentieth.

3. This painting is generally called *Vuillard and Varoqui*. In his journals, Vuillard cites his friend's name as "Waroquy," and that spelling will be used here.

4. Vuillard mentions Waroquy in: EV I.1, 16v (28 November 1888); EV I.1, 20 (1 December 1888); EV I.1, 22 (4 December 1888); and EV I.1, 23v (6 December 1888).

In EV I.2, 44v (16 July 1894) Vuillard mentions running into Waroquy's girlfriend and talking about old memories: "Recontré à Notre Dame l'amie de Waroquy vieux souvenirs." This indicates that by 1894 Vuillard and Waroquy were no longer close friends.

5. Given the large scale of the painting in The Metropolitan Museum of Art, it is likely that Vuillard is referring to this painting in his journal. A separate study for Waroquy's head exists, slightly more specific in detail than in the double portrait. But there is also a small picture of Waroquy (Huguette Berès, Paris) painted in brilliant colors, with quite a different effect than the one we see here. For the entire contents of the chronologies Vuillard wrote, please refer to Appendix A.

6. Several sketches exist of a girl with a pony tail, and there is a beautiful painting from about 1892 that depicts two girls walking, both with similar braids. Yet when Vuillard paints Marie as a seamstress or in scenes with his mother, she is identifiable by her hunched over pose and the chignon on top of her head.

7. There are several versions of this episode, often using different colors in the example. Linda Nochlin, in *Impressionism and Post-Impressionism, 1874–1904, Sources and Documents in the History of Art* (Englewood Cliffs, New Jersey: Prentice-Hall, Inc., 1966), p. 181, cites the version recounted by Agnes Humbert, *Les Nabis et leur époque: 1888–1900* (Geneva: P. Cailler, 1954), p. 30. Bogomila Welsh-Ovcharov is closer to the source in citing Denis's account of the episode which he published in *L'Occident* in 1903: "L'Influence de Paul Gauguin." (Reprinted in Maurice Denis, *Théories, 1890–1910: Du Symbolisme et de Gauguin vers un nouvel ordre classique*, Paris: Bibliothèque de L'Occident, 1912, p. 167.) That text reads as: "How do you see this tree, is it truly green? Then put on some green, the most beautiful green of your palette; and this shadow—rather blue? Don't be afraid to paint it as blue as possible."

Mary-Anne Stevens, in *Post-Impressionism*, exh. cat. (London: Royal Academy of Art, 1980), p. 128, makes the important point that *The Talisman* was still a landscape painted from life, rather than from memory. She adds that Sérusier had been contemplating the relationship between nature and memory in 1889, and that this led Denis to hesitate from advocating complete abstraction in his "Définition du néo-traditionnisme" of 1890. Vuillard, too, had been wrestling with the idea of memory early on: "Essai de peindre de memoire." See Appendix A, entries for 1889.

8. EV I.1, 12 (22 November 1888):

Nous percevons la nature par les sens qui nous donnent les images de formes et de couleurs, de son, etc. une forme une couleur n'existe que par rapport à une autre . . .

9. EV I.1, 71–71v (31 August 1890):

Corot, un accent dans quelque chose de flou dan un accord parfait de gris nombreux un son. (à propos d'une étude pastel de gris clair 2 tons purs un de rouge l'autre de vert . . . alors les tableaux de corot sont toujours uniquement une symphonie de gris avec un seul ton différent.

10. Maurice Denis, "Définition du néo-traditionnisme," *Art et critique* (August 1890), translated in Nochlin, p. 187. Denis, in turn, also felt a debt to Sérusier. In Denis's preface to his *Théories*, he credits Sérusier, "qui a éveillé en moi le sens des théories . . . sur la metaphysique et l'art, en 1888, à l'Académie Julian." It was Sérusier who brought "la bonne nouvelle des idées de Gauguin" and who instigated the Nabi gatherings, which included the core group of Bonnard, H. G. Ibels, René Piot, Paul Ranson, Roussel, Vuillard, and Denis. Denis mentions that later additions to the group included Rippl-Ronnai, Rasetti, Jean Verkade, Georges Lacombe, and lastly Vallotton and Maillol (*Théories*, p. vi). The catalogue *The Nabis and the Parisian Avant-Garde* (New Brunswick, N.J.: Helen Voorhees Zimmerli Art Museum, Rutgers University, 1988, Patricia Eckert Boyer, ed.), which was published as this book went to press, outlines the activities and contributions of lesser-known members of the group, such as the Danish Mogens Ballin and the Scottish James Pitcairn-Knowles.

11. EV I.2, 71v (31 August 1890):

. . . concevoir bien un tableau comme un ensemble d'accords, s'éloignant définitivement d'idée naturaliste.

12. EV I.2, 20 (6 September 1890):

Expression *pur et simple* venant purement et simplement des lignes et des couleurs de la chose elle-même parbleu, de la peinture et pas des idées associées.

13. EV I.2, 23v (24 October 1890):

Ainsi l'expression objective doit seule importer . . . l'expression des lignes et des taches (ne pas vouloir imaginer l'expression subjective des lignes et des taches) De la . . . renoncement à une oeuvre définitive immédiate (nous ne sommes même pas des primitifs!) mais calme et beauté de l'esprit de Sérusier!) Peut-être rapidement si j'ai le courage d'appliquer ces idées!

Objective expression of interior states was also the essence of Gustave Kahn's famous comments of September 1886 from *L'Evénement*: "Our art's essential aim is to objectify the subjective (the exteriorization of the idea), instead of subjectifying the objective (nature seen through a temperament)." It should be remembered that both Sérusier and Denis refer to Zola's comment about nature with which Kahn parenthetically concludes. Sérusier writes about "temperament" in the *ABC de la peinture* as a physiological explanation for everything that discounted the psychic influence; Denis referred to it directly in the "Définition," discounting it as vague.

14. The notion of the primitive is not the focus of our argument here or of Vuillard's writings, except for this one reference. Denis wrote about primitivism in his "Définition," referring to the Italians:

> J'avoue que *les predelles* del l'Angelico qui est au Louvre, *l'Homme en rouge* de Ghirlandaio et nombre d'autres oeuvres des primitifs, me rappellent plus precisement la "nature" que Giorgione, Raphael, le Vinci. C'est un autre manière de voir,—ce sont des fantasies différentes. (*Théories,* p. 3.)

The idea that primitive art revealed deep human truths is what encouraged the Nabis' curiosity about Italian trecento painting. Two unpublished letters reveal the excitement that two Nabis felt when uncovering the work of these "primitives" that was not represented in the Louvre at all. The first letter, dated 1892, was sent to Vuillard from Mogens Ballin, a relatively unknown Danish painter who briefly was part of the Nabi circle in Paris and who helped to exhibit their work in his native country.

> Siena, 4 décembre 1892
>
> Mon cher ami!
>
> Bien souvent j'ai eu l'intention de vous remercier mais vous savez comme c'est difficile a écrire ces choses la, . . . vous étiez le premier à faire disparaître les folies synthe-symbos, etc, etc, de mon horizon. Les maîtres Italiens ont fait la reste . . . Oui, oui j'admire les maîtres Raphael, Leonardo, Botticelli etc. mais j'aime les primitifs surtout ceux de Siena bien d'avantage—ils sont tellement superbes que Fra Angelico entre eux est de 4ème 5ème rang. Louvre donne en vérité une bien faible idée de l'art du XIII, XIIIIe siècle. Tel que Buoninsegna (par Siena), dont tu ignores probablement le nom, fait dans une suite de petits tableaux d'une savoureuse coloration . . .
>
> Mogens Ballin

The second letter, from Maurice Denis, was probably written during his trip to Italy in 1895.

> Mon cher Vuillard,
>
> C'est Assise . . . Il y a des merveilleuses choses de Giotto et de tous ses élèves . . . Je reviens enthousiasme des vrais primitifs, ceux qu'on ne voit pas à Paris, les merveilleux peintres de fresques, depuis Cimabue, Giotto sur tout, c'est le maître de l'art classique jusqu'à l'Angelico, capanant (?) par les Gaddi, Memmi, l'Orcagna, Spinelli, Giovanni da Milano, Andrea da Firenze, des inconnus.

15. EV I.2, 19v (before 6 September 1890):

> . . . plaisent par les accords de tons et le dessin exterieur et non par le plus ou moins d'exactitude avec laquelle elles rappellent leurs modèles qui nous sont inconnus. Difficulté de bien établir ça dans ma tête après les longues heures passées il y a deux ans devant ces toiles imbues d'idées naturalistes, ne m'apercevant pas qu'entre ces idées de copie d'alors et ces plaisirs pur et simple de ces harmonies de ton, il n'y avait aucun rapport . . . Rien n'est important que l'état d'âme dans lequel on est pour pouvoir assujetir sa penser à une sensation ne penser qu'à elle tout en cherchant le moyen d'expression.

16. EV I.2, 19v (before 6 September 1890):

> Impression innouie des dessins de Denis; la grande sagesse sera quand je verrai ces oeuvres sans retour sur moi-même et comparaison immediate; toute autre expression je puis rendre (je viens de faire une jeune femme fraiche courant dans les lignes prudhomesque que n'a pas Denis; mais ce qui me manque c'est l'assurance et le travail continue qui en est la conscience.

17. EV I.2, 20 (6 September 1890):

> Penser à l'effet produit par les oeuvres des autres; il faut regarder ces oeuvres comme celles des autres pour en avoir une impression et juger de leur expression.

18. EV I.2, 30v-31 (March 1891):

> J'ai envie de faire une . . . avec une ancienne académie. Pourquoi: En feuilletant ces vieilles études j'ai été frappé de l'expression de quelques unes rares qui n'avait pas été trop détruites par le souci de rendre les différentes parties de l'objet representé . . . d'abord pour employer les mots d'autrefois l'académie en question est plus d'ensemble autrement dit elle forme un *tout*; alors tous les éléments employés sont harmonieux à ce tout . . . (puisque je ne les considèrais plus comme *détails*, un détail étant la *partie* d'un tout et en art la partie harmonieuse d'un tout) Alors l'ensemble n'est plus un ensemble c'est une feuille de papier couverte d'un tas d'éléments disparates; c['est] à d[ire] ayant chacun une expression différente l'ensembles ne peut donc en avoir une puissante. Il n'y a donc pas à se dire devant cette académie pour en faire un tableau, je vais en faire un Ingres, un Delacroix, ou un Rembrandt, laissons nous aller à l'émotion qu'elle me donne, les lignes ou les taches que je poserai sur une toile seront de moi.

19. EV I.2, 30v (March 1891):

> Le sujet d'une oeuvre quelconque est une émotion simple et naturelle à l'auteur.

20. EV I.2, 33 (2 April 1891):

> L'observation pure et simple est un *fait* acte de vie simple et c'est cette simple et primitive observation qui est nécessaire, qui *est*. Si donc nous étions des êtres simples, et non . . . gâtés par des préjugés et des habitudes, nos oeuvres seraient facilement belles parce qu'il n'y aurait pas de lutte pour distinguer la vérité du mensonge. Alors devant une oeuvre d'art il ne faut pas se demander si telle théorie est appliquée, mais est elle belle? Pourtant l'on dit une belle couleur une belle ligne et oui vous suivez un moment d'émotion sur cette couleur sur cette ligne qui synthèse Tout à ce moment. Maintenant un tableau par exemple ce n'est pas telle couleur ou telle forme, c'est l'ensemble de ces couleurs ou de ces formes . . .

21. EV I.2, 31 (March 1891):

> Il ne faut lui [Sérusier] prendre ses théories qu'en tant que théories et non sa façon de les appliquer; ainsi lui quand il trace des lignes . . . il sait à quelle idée théorique il obéit; il ne faut pas l'imiter en songeant à l'expression seule que donne son oeuvre.

Maurice Denis also discussed the idea of beauty in his "Définition," indicating that it was a totally subjective assessment: "Avant d'exterioriser ses sensations telles quelles, it faudrait en déterminer la valeur, au point de vue de la beauté." (*Théories,* p. 3.)
   Vuillard's ideas of both beauty and harmony might have been derived from Charles Blanc's *Grammaire des arts du dessin* (Paris, 1867), which was a basic text for all students at the Ecole des Beaux-Arts. Blanc writes about the order of beauty as opposed to the chaos of the sublime: "Le sublime peut donc se trouver partout, même dans le chaos, même dans l'horrible; le beau ne saurait être conçu en dehors de certaines lois d'ordre, de proportion de l'harmonie." (p. 66.)

22. EV I.2, 43v (15 July 1894):

> En peinture n'est-ce pas de même l'évocation de ces images interieurs par des moyens très generaux aussi, couleurs et formes. L'art consiste à introduire un ordre dans ces moyens suggestifs de ces images.

23. An earlier work in this series was formerly in the collection of Mr. and Mrs. Leigh B. Block. Vuillard paints himself in similarly abstract forms but with a much paler, more neutral palette.

24. The allusion to halos in van Gogh's work would not have been out of keeping with Vuillard's own deeply religious sentiments. Vuillard writes on 24 October 1890 (EV I.2, 24): "Dieu formule de toute harmonie de toute intelligence qui nous pénètre partout qui nous entoure de vos signes . . . plus d'orgeuil humain, fierté seule et légitime de participer à l'universelle harmonie, d'être fils de Dieu!"

25. EV I.2, 74 (after 31 August 1890):

> Chose remarquable dans les musées et l'histoire de la peinture, plus les
> peintres sont mystiques plus leurs couleurs sont vives (rouges bleus
> jaunes). . .

Icons of Inwardness: The Sewing Paintings

Je n'ai jamais vécu qu'avec des femes dans les endroits d'où je tirais mes sujets
EV I.2, 47 (27 July 1894)

1. Andrew Carduff Ritchie, *Edouard Vuillard* (New York: The Museum of
Modern Art, 1954), p. 8; and John Russell, *Vuillard* (London: Thames and
Hudson, 1971), p. 12. The confusion over Mme. Vuillard's profession is
easily explained: as I note below, the paintings would seem to indicate that
dresses, rather than smaller items such as corsets, were her stock in trade.

2. The French text of the letter is as follows:

Paris, le ————187——

Corsets et Orthopédie
Brevets SGDG

Mme. Vuillard
Successeur
Rue Nve. St. Augustin, 60
près de l'Opéra

Madame

J'ai l'honneur de vous prévenir que depuis le 15 avril j'exploite pour mon
comte la maison de fabrication de Corsets de Mme. Duval-Caron, 60 rue
Nve. St. Augustin.

    J'espère, Madame, que vous voudrez bien me continuer votre confiance,
je mettrai tous mes soins à vous satisfaire.

    Dans l'espoir de votre prochaine visite, agréez, Madame, mes salutations
distingués.

H. Vuillard

Many printed copies of this letter exist as Vuillard used it as paper for his
journals during the years 1890 to 1905; he would simply write over the
printed text or use the verso. It should be noted that the letter was signed
"H. Vuillard." Vuillard's mother's name was Marie Justine, his father's
Joseph François Honoré, so one would assume that the "H." refers to
Monsieur, rather than Madame, Vuillard. The implications of this are
unclear, as we know that Monsieur Vuillard was not the corsetmaker.

3. See, for instance, Jacques Salomon, *Vuillard: témoignage* (Paris: Michel,
1945), pp. 10–11: "Ses maigres rentes et la modeste pension de son mari
decidèrent Mme. Vuillard à entreprendre un commerce de modes en ap-
partement."

4. "Nous verrons si comme vous le dites nous pouvons definitivement nous
entendre." The letter is in the Salomon family archives.

5. It should be noted that the corporation of *couturières*, which was also
established at this time and which consisted of *les couturières en habit, en
corps d'enfant, en linge*, and *en garniture*, expected its members to have a
three-year apprenticeship and a training of two years before the "maitrise"
for the "chef d'oeuvre." See Léon de Seilhac, *L'Industrie de la couture et de la
confection à Paris* (Paris, 1897), p. 3.

6. See Mme. P. Lebrun, "Corsetière de de Raincy, Banlieu de Paris: veuve
travaillant à domicile avec ses enfants, ouvrière à la tâche, proprietaire," In
Les ouvriers des deux mondes (La Societé d'économie sociale, 3e série, 15e
fascicule, 1905), p. 418. This case study offers a detailed account of the
corset trade.

7. Lebrun, p. 418.

8. Lebrun, p. 419.

9. Seilhac, pp. 13–14.

10. Ernest Léoty, *Le corset à travers les ages* (Paris, 1893).

11. Archives de la Seine; Archives des Direction de l'Enregistrement. It
should be mentioned that her husband left nothing to his heirs either. One
can assume that when there is no *inventaire après décès,* nothing of value
belonged to the deceased. There is no information relating to the where-
abouts of papers concerning Mme. Vuillard's corset business other than the
previously cited letter from Mme. Duval-Caron. Because only real estate
purchases had to be notarized, it is likely that facts regarding Mme.
Vuillard's purchase of the business, as well as her income, will never be
known. Likewise, no documents have come to light regarding the sale of
Mme. Vuillard's business upon her retirement.

12. Octave Festy, Ministère du Travail et de la prévoyance sociale, Office
du travail, *Enquête sur le travail à domicile dans l'industrie de la lingerie* (Paris,
1907–1911), p. x.

The industry of "lingerie" includes corsets. This favorable account of the
position of the worker in this industry is at odds with all the other
contemporary accounts examined, but the fact that this version comes from
the official branch of the government might account for the positive tone:

> . . . depuis quelques annés, le luxe de la lingerie et des vêtements de dessous,
> jupes, chemisettes, cache-corset, a pris un developpement extrême, très favor-
> able à l'industrie de la lingerie parisienne . . . Cette production exception-
> nellement grande de lingerie a été surtout profitable aux ouvrières. La main-
> d'oeuvre a sensiblement hausse et, à certains moments, elle est devenue
> introuvable. Cette hausse da la façon, jointe à celle des tissus de coton, a
> enlevé aux fabricants une faible partie de leurs benefices sur les objets de
> lingerie de femme, cependant très recherchés, et a rendu les affaires très
> difficiles pour la lingerie d'homme, dans laquelle les marges de benefice sont
> très limités.
>
> L'exportation a sensiblement augmenté depuis quelques annés, sans avoir
> regagné le niveau d'il y a quinze ans.
>
> Exportation des pièces de lingeries cousues:

	kg	francs
1905	607,800	24,767,700
1890	1,112,000	59,715,474

13. Seilhac, pp. 56–57. The breakdown was as follows: 996 *couturières,*
261 *modistes,* 80 *brodeuses,* 37 *corsetières,* 21 *fleuristes ou plumassières.*

14. See Seilhac, p. 25:

> les avantages materiels d'institutions corporatives, des bureaux de placement,
> de contentieux, de reseignement, une caisse de prêts gratuits, une caisse
> d'encouragement aux sociétés de secours mutuels, une maison de famille pour
> les ouvrières isolées, les soins gratuits d'un medecin.

15. It is not entirely clear what this figure actually is doing in the picture.
Her hands are at either side of what might be a plate instead of material,
her head bent while saying grace instead of sewing. Nonetheless, the pose
recalls that of other women sewing.
    The depiction of features using a few lines of paint in the most minimal
way is similar to the economic technique employed by Hokusai in his
woodblock compendium *Mangwa.*

16. A preliminary sketch related to this painting was formerly with J.P.L.
Fine Arts, London. The same untouched area near the torso is visible in the
sketch, but its meaning is no more clear in the drawing than in the
painting.

17. Colta Ives noticed this combination of techniques in the lithograph. She suggested that this reflected the way fabrics were printed, referring to the fact that Vuillard's mother's family, the Michauds, had been in the textile business. Colta Ives, *The Great Wave: The Influence of Japanese Woodcuts on French Prints,* exh. cat. (New York: The Metropolitan Museum of Art, 1974), p. 69.

18. This painting has been dated circa 1898 because of the likeness of the pose to that of Mme. Vuillard in *La Cuisinière* from Vuillard's series of lithographs *Paysages et interieurs* of that same year. However, given that Vuillard used figures in the same pose over a period of years, sometimes using for his compositions sketches from his journal dating several years before the actual painting, to date this picture as late as 1898 is unwarranted. The simplicity of the composition would more likely link the picture to others painted in the middle of the decade.

19. Lebrun. Startling similarities exist between the subject of the article, a "Mme. G," and Mme. Vuillard. "Mme. G" worked on the rue Daunou, as did Mme. Vuillard from 1878 to 1886, and both women were widows of career army men. M. Vuillard retired from service in 1859 because of wounds received in Africa; "M. G's" career ended after he was wounded in the Franco-Prussian war. Both women had three children; in each case one of the children stayed at home to live with the mother. While their life patterns are similar, the precise roles the women played in the corset business are different. "Mme. G" was employed by a *corsetière sur mesure,* whose business might have been on the scale of Mme. Vuillard's. Thus her salary could not be comparable to Mme. Vuillard's earnings. Further, "Mme. G" did not live in the neighborhood. She moved to the suburbs of Paris, thirteen kilometers away, in order to enable a daughter of delicate health to live in the fresh country air. There she could also supplement the family income by growing vegetables and raising chickens, rabbits, and pigeons.

20. Lebrun, p. 398.

> Les corsets confiés a l'ouvrière sont coupés, batis pour l'assemblage ou même déjà piqués. Ils ont subi un premier essayage et les rectifications sont faites ou indiquées par des épingles.
>
> Rentrée chez elle, l'ouvrière pique le corset, s'il ne l'est pas déjà; elle le monte, le bride, l'entoure, le rabat, batit et pique les galons ou les rubans dans lesquelles elle enfile les baleines. Elle les arrête, pose le busc et les ressorts, éventaille le corset, le borde, met les coussins s'il en faut, et pose les garnitures. Les corsets sont livré sans les oeillets qui sont posés chez la patronne. Les corsets sont quelquefois doublés, et la doublure se pose presque en dernier lieu.

21. Lebrun, p. 387. Certain facts and figures, of course, would have been different in Mme. Vuillard's day. It should also be remembered that the *corsetière* in the study worked for someone else, while Mme. Vuillard had her own business, and that the former lived outside Paris, while Vuillard's mother lived in the heart of the city.

22. This working schedule is not peculiar to those in the corset trade. Henriette Vanier, in her chapter on the working woman from her book, *La mode et ses métiers, frivolités et luttes des classes, 1830–1870* (Paris, 1890), includes a passage from *L'Opinion des Femmes* from 1849. It describes a similar situation five decades before the one described here:

> On engage les ouvrières pour la saison d'été au mois de mars et pour la saison d'hiver au mois de septembre. La saison d'été finit à la fin de mai, et celle d'hiver en janvier pour les chapeaux et en février pour les parures de bal. Bien qu'on engage les ouvrières pour l'année, on renvoie néanmoins à la fin de chaque saison celles dont on n'a pas été satisfait, et on occupe les autres comme on peut . . . Mais quand la bonne saison revient . . . les journées commencent à 9 heures et finnissent à 11 heures, minuit, heureuses sont les pauvres enfants quand il ne faut pas veiller plusieurs nuits par semaine et travailler le dimanche. (p. 86.)

Seilhac mentions that before the law of 2 November 1892, the legal working day was twelve hours. He also adds that the greatest irregularity in working hours reigns in the clothing industry because the industry is so dependent on the whims and seasons of its clientele (p. 34).

The law of 1892 improved the situation of the workers in the clothing industry. Before then, the couture houses could demand "la veillée" of their workers, which meant that everyone in the atelier would have to stay and work from 7:30 at night until sometimes after 1:00 a.m. The problem was compounded when the worker could not return home at that late hour because there was no means of transportation. So they often stayed in the ateliers and slept on their chairs, only to begin work again the next morning.

The law of 2 November 1892 stated that these late night sessions could not continue after 11 p.m. By 1893 other specifications had been introduced whereby only workers older than eighteen could stay late, and even they could not be required to do this more than sixty days a year.

In 1897 the legal working day for those under sixteen could not surpass ten hours; workers between the ages of sixteen and eighteen could not work more than eleven hours, under the condition that the total weekly hours did not surpass sixty hours. The weekly maximum was sixty-six hours for those over eighteen. (Seilhac, p. 38.)

23. Lebrun, p. 389.

24. Stéphane Mallarmé, "Réponse à des enquêtes: Sur l'évolution littéraire," in *Oeuvres complètes* (Paris: Editions Gallimard, 1945), pp. 868–69.

25. EV I.2, 75 (August 1893):

> Pourquoi est-ce dans les lieux familiers que l'esprit et la sensibilité trouvent le plus de véritablement nouveau? le nouveau est toujours nécessaire à la vie, à la conscience.

26. Louis Emile Edmond Duranty, *La Nouvelle peinture* (Paris, 1876), as translated in Charles S. Moffett, ed., *The New Painting: Impressionism 1874–1886* (Geneva: Richard Burton SA and San Francisco: The Fine Arts Museums of San Francisco, 1986), p. 44. Although Duranty's essay is well known because of its importance to the Naturalists and to the new vision of Edgar Degas, it also had a profound effect on Vuillard. He was so devoted to the essay that he was instrumental in bringing about its republication in 1944. For more on the importance of Duranty to Vuillard's art, see Russell, pp. 18–19.

27. It has been proposed that this painting was created as a design for a ceramic tile, which would account for the unusually flat and monochromatic shapes of the seamstresses. See Belinda Thompson, *Vuillard* (New York: Abbeville, 1988), p. 32.

28. EV I.2, 24 (24 October 1890):

> Exprimons ce que je sens (c'est une simple désignation, un *fait* pur et simple de désigner la chose que j'ai dans la tête): une expression d'attendrissement causé par tel objet (les 2 sont l'expression objective) plutôt expression de grandeur et une pyramide (un objet que là—à qui je donnerai aura ce caractère). puis je trace sur le papier d'un coup comme on parle net quand une idée se présente) la ligne ou la tache imaginée et voulue je la développe si besoin est je compose fait simple en lui-même composer et toute ma patience (oh alors cela est facile) est absorbé par le souci de bien *faire* et alors possibilité de travail manuel vraiment très prolongé.

29. Vuillard shared a studio with Pierre Bonnard, Maurice Denis, and the playwright Lugné-Poë beginning in 1891. A painting by Bonnard shows the model, identically posed, from a slightly different angle. See Pierre Bonnard, *Catalogue Raisonné de l'oeuvre Peint* (Paris: J. et H. Bernheim, 1966–1974), vol. 4, no. 01712.

30. EV I.2, 20v (6 September 1890):

. . . une tête de femme vient me donner certaine émotion, cette émotion seule doit me servir et je ne dois pas chercher à me souvenir du nez ou de l'oreille, cela n'importe en rien. . .

31. Albert Aurier, quoted in John Rewald, *Post-Impressionism* (New York: The Museum of Modern Art, 3rd ed., 1978), pp. 481–82.

Several months after the publication of this groundbreaking article, Vuillard responded to some of Aurier's ideas in his journal:

Ce plaisir décoratif, ces harmonies sont les signes qui s'imposent, on ne doit pas y trouver un plaisir uniquement q[uel]q[ue] chose de séparé de l'idée c'[est] à d[ire] une affection des sens. Seulement ce sont ces sens qui communiquent l'idée dans sa vérité et sa beauté—Toute oeuvre est l'Objet d'une Idée. Mais l'Auteur en a-t-il toujours conscience. Des ébauches, des avortements sont toujours objets par conséquent suggèrent des Idées. Mais un véritable Travail digne de ce nom sera toujours idéaliste parce qu'il sera conscient de l'Idée. L'auteur le verra. (EV I.2, 86, September 1891)

32. EV I.2, 30 (March 1891):

Et chose admirable, l'Esprit qui devrait dans notre cas être toujours le plus fort, devient l'esclave des sens; on veut *sentir*, ou plutôt on ne fait cas que de l'émotion, et quand il s'agit de réfléchir, de généraliser de symboliser, on reste impuissant; on croit à l'existence d'un symbole spécial, partiel. . .

Thus far he appears to be summarizing Aurier, but then his argument departs when he continues:

mais il n'est symbole que par rapport à l'ensemble de nos opérations spirituelles! I! faut de toute nécessité pour vivre, (cette oeuvre) il faut un ensemble rythmique; solide de conviction, de foi . . . sorte de clef qui permette de comprendre les signes.

33. Anne Georges, in her thesis "Symbolisme et décor: Vuillard 1888–1905" (3e cycle, Paris I, 1978) states that before 1893 Vuillard's compositions were essentially flat.

34. Vuillard painted a portrait of Mme. Michaud in this room: *Portrait of the Artist's Grandmother* (fig. 49). The same vertical strip of circles is a visible wall decoration in both pictures.

35. Ursula Perucchi-Petri mentions this as well. See *Die Nabis und Japan* (Munich: Prestel-Verlag, 1976), p. 103.

36. Perucchi-Petri, p. 103. André Chastel, "Vuillard," *Art News Annual*, vol. 23 (1954), p. 47, attributes this roving perspective to the influence of the theater, where the eye cuts across the stage at angles that open and close space. He also observes that artificial light plays a strong role in this picture and attributes this influence to Degas. There are close connections between Degas's and Vuillard's work, both in their paintings of working women and in their depiction of pictorial space. This picture owes two clear debts to Degas: the use of silhouette for the figure and the flattening of space by creating a fluid area of unmodulated background. Here the left side of the canvas displays an uninterrupted passage from wall to floor, extending from the top to the bottom of the picture. As in Degas's dance pictures where large expanses of the floor take up a great deal of the foreground, Vuillard also enhances this spatial flattening. In this painting there is nothing to indicate that the floor comes toward the viewer.

37. The light cast by the lamp appears to create a separate brown decoration, not a highlight, on the sleeve of the woman to the left.

38. As this book went to press, Patricia Eckert Boyer published an essay, "The Nabis, Parisian Humorous Illustrations, and the Chat Noir," in *The Nabis and the Parisian Avant-Garde* (New Brunswick, N.J.: Helen Voorhees Zimmerli Art Museum, Rutgers University, 1988), pp. 1–79. Boyer links the silhouette to the shadow theater of the Chat Noir. Her argument provides interesting comparative material for paintings by Vuillard such as *L'Aiguillée*.

39. Perucchi-Petri, p. 114.

40. EV I.2, 66 (January 1894):

Etonnante chose qu'un Chéret à côté d'un Lautrec. Parce qu'un dessin est plus ou moins noir et que les traits en sont plus ou moins gros ce n'est pas une raison pour qu'il soit plus ou moins significatif.

41. EV I:1 (25 November 1888)

42. Perucchi-Petri (p. 97) links this early exposure to Japonism to the Synthetist exhibition at the Café Volpini in 1889, where Vuillard would have seen Gauguin's Japanese-inspired works, and the exhibition of Japanese woodcuts at the Ecole des Beaux-Arts that same year.

43. Thadée Natanson, "Exposition Hiroshighe et Outamaro," *La Revue Blanche*, vol. 4 (1893), pp. 140–44.

. . . la plupart des éstampes n'ont q'un sujet très simple ou pas de sujet, puis qu'il leur suffit d'une attitude de femme, de deux femmes côté à côté, d'une mère et son bébé.

De ces femmes et de ces enfants c'est moins le visage ou le corps que la parrure qui a retenu l'artiste . . . Il a suffi du trait pour indiquer la ligne du nez, l'arc des yeux; . . . la modèle ou la couleur de la chair. Outamaro a poussé autrement loin la recherche de la valeur ornementale et décorative des lignes et des couleurs, établi patiemment la signification des formes.

Ainsi, dans cet enfant et cette femme attachant la moustiquaire, les corps et les visages sont à peine indiquées, comme laissés de côté et le merveilleux savoir faire du peintre ne s'est amusé qu'à pousser les tons de la chevelure noire, de la ceinture noire à liséré d'or, du réseau vert des mailles, de la petite robe de l'enfant, et à chercher jusqu'à la minutie la forme des détails, plis drapés, cheveux tordus, dessin ornemental des étoffes.

C'est surtout ce volontaire allongement pictural des lignes ou l'harmonie des courbes qui donnent la grace et l'élégance, l'arrangement de composition qui fait le charme et, la somptuosité décorative, les miroirs ou les fards, la coquetterie.

Mais elle se préoccupe chez Outamaro, negligeant un visage pour achever une ceinture, surtout de la valeur ornementale et décorative des formes, les aime et s'y attache pour elles-mêmes, pour la signification picturale des tous et du dessin. Les couleurs déclat aigu ou de douceur comme endormie, il ne les a juxtaposées que pour la joie de leurs qualités ou de leurs valeurs propres et l'interêt de leurs rapports. Elles n'ont ainsi, presque exclusivement, qu'un sens pictural, comme elles n'ont qu'une harmonie plastique, sans autre intention. La même aspect caractérise la composition du dessin. Et, s'il semble avoir plus volontairement élancé ou courbé les lignes pour un effet de grace ou d'élégance, c'est à peine si la fantaisie de son intention dépassé l'exclusive préoccupation ornementale. Il n'a si amoureusement et patiemment étudié ces formes jusqu'à la minutie que pour exprimer leur signification décorative.

44. In fact, a lithograph by Vuillard shows an atelier of seamstresses with two windows. See Claude Roger-Marx, *L'Oeuvre gravé de Vuillard* (Paris and Monte Carlo: Sauret, 1948), p. 50, no. 14.

45. EV I.1, 55v (7 September 1890):

à creuser l'idée que j'ai déjà suffisamment de quoi m'occuper des années entières à développer et utiliser *mettre en oeuvres d'art* tout ce que j'ai dans mes cahiers et cartons.

46. Although Perucchi-Petri refers to this panel as a screen (pp. 106–108), the square doorknob makes its identity clear.

47. This extreme roundness could also be a drop leaf that has been left folded down, but because Vuillard did not indicate the joint, the round table appears skewed toward the viewer.

48. Stuart Preston, *Vuillard* (New York: Abrams, 1971), p. 76; *Edouard Vuillard, Ker-Xavier Roussel*, exh. cat. (Paris: Orangerie des Tuileries, 1968), p. 75; and Jacques Salomon, *Vuillard admiré* (Lausanne, 1961), p. 40.

137

49. EV I.2, 46–46v (27 July 1894).

Dans les aspects que je choisis quand soi-disant j'observe, pour en tirer des sujets de peinture ou de méditation de peinture je constate quoique jusqu'ici je n'aie guère assemblé, composé si l'on veut, que des *tâches* assez informes, malgré la croyance, qui n'est qu'une duperie et un manque de réflexion sur moi-même, que je suis indifférent aux objets présentés aux yeux, je devrais avoir une multitude variée d'objets représentés dans mes peintures, or je n'introduis jamais de personnages hommes, je constate. D'autre part quand mon attention se porte sur les hommes, je vois toujours d'infames charges, je n'ai qu'un sentiment d'objets ridicules. Jamais devant les femmes où je trouve toujours moyen d'isoler quelques éléments qui satisfont en moi le peintre. Or les uns ne sont pas plus laids que les autres ils ne le sont que dans mon imagination.

50. This piece resembles a chest in two other paintings of the atelier, *Mme. Vuillard au chiffonnier* and *Les Ouvrières au chiffonnier*. See *Vuillard*, exh. cat. (Frankfurt: Frankfurter Kunstverein, 1964), cat. nos. 19 and 3.

51. These windows are also visible in a painting titled *The Open Door* (Frankfurt, 1964, cat. no. 13).

52. Lebrun, p. 389.

53. Lebrun, p. 291.

54. Lebrun, p. 393. The inquiry on the *Corsetière de Raincy* reaches to such an extent that all the items of furniture are listed for each room. The dining room reveals its dual function as both a work and a social space, for it includes:

un buffet, une table + six chaises en noyer, machine à coudre, une table à ouvarage + un autre table. Un tapis recouvre la table principale, la cheminée est garnie de legers bibelots, quelques chromos ornent les murs. Un tapis en linoleum, placé sous la table, protège le parquet très soigneusement encaustique, la fenêtre est garnie de rideaux de guipure et de doubles rideaux confectionnés par les filles cette fenêtre s'ouvre sur le jardin fleuri.

Chacune a sa place marquée dans cette pièce qui est bien plus la salle de travail que la salle à manger.

Mere: Machine è coudre. La grande table pour retoucher et apprêter.

Fille ainée: la table à ouvrage, tout près de la fenêtre et tournée de façon à ce que la lumière tombe facilement sur le travail, sans faux mouvements, sans fatigue inutile du corps.

Plus jeune fille: N'a pas besoin de tant de ménagements. Elle est moins assidue aux travaux de couture, qu'elle remplace par les soins du ménage et de la basse-cour.

Le dimache, les utensiles de travail font place aux assiettes, aux couverts et aux plats copieusement garnis, autour desquelles se réunit la famille.

Although specific details are known about several of Vuillard's apartments, notably those of the rue du Marché St. Honoré and the rue Truffaut, both of which are extant, little specific information remains about the apartments on the rue St. Honoré, where Vuillard painted these scenes.

The 1862 and 1876 cadastral surveys of Paris (*Calepins cadastres*), now housed in the Archives de la Seine, include thorough descriptions of each building in Paris and an update of its occupants. Through this resource one can discover the size of Vuillard's apartments and the specific descriptions of the buildings in which they were located. For further information on Vuillard's apartments, see "The Drama of Daily Life."

55. The six panels, commissioned by cousins of Vuillard's friends Misia and Thadée Natanson, made up Vuillard's first large-scale decorative ensemble. See Russell, pp. 34–35.

56. It should be added that he only seldom included references to actual work being done on a sewing machine. While Vuillard's scenes of sewing recall his mother's atelier and the personal effects that surround the quotidian aspects of the corset trade, later images of sewing refer much more to the mechanized elements involved. For example. both Umberto Boccioni and Fernand Léger painted images of women sewing that date to the first decade of the twentieth century. In *La Cucitrice*, dated 1908, Boccioni combined the soft outline of a sewing machine with the profile of a seated woman silhouetted by the light that filters in from a window. Yet she is reading not sewing. Other images by Boccioni, *Due vecchie sedute*, dated 1907, for example, recall Vuillard so closely in both subject matter and stylistic execution that one wonders if Boccioni might have seen a reproduced lithograph. Léger's painting of a woman sewing becomes in itself the mechanized image, as Robert Rosenblum states:

His [Léger's] treatment of the genre theme of a woman sewing is aggressively contemporary. Not only has the woman herself been joined together out of simple blocks and cylinders, as one would construct a machine, but her implied movements of hand and arm have a comparably regular and automatic quality . . . one is tempted to retitle Léger's painting "Sewing Machine." (*Cubism and Twentieth Century Art*, New York: Abrams, 1960, p. 126.)

I would like to thank Emily Braun for bringing some of these references to my attention.

The Drama of Daily Life: The Family Portraits

Ainsi cette idée de la vie qui nous entoure de notre vie, source de toutes nos réflexions et productions, cela devient le modernisme . . .
EV I.2, 51 (26 October 1894)

1. Salomon, *Vuillard admiré*, p. 30.

2. Ursula Perucchi-Petri has linked this pose to those frequently found in Japanese prints.

3. EV I.2, 50v (26 October 1894):

on vit entouré d'objets *ornés*. dans l'intérieur le plus ordinaire il n'y a pas un objet dont la forme n'ait une prétention ornementale, la plupart du temps elle nous cache, cette forme, sa raison d'être, sous des agréments étrangers.

Vuillard would pursue his decorative manipulations of lamps in his lithograph series *Paysages et intérieurs*. In three of the scenes, *Intérieur à la suspension, Intérieur aux teintures roses I,* and *Intérieur aux teintures roses II,* lamps play a major role. But even though this series was completed several years after Vuillard painted *The Vuillard Family at Lunch*, he uses a similar lamp in *Intérieur aux teintures roses II*, this time with more emphasis on the whole object, to block the head of a woman in a checked dress who stands to the extreme left of the composition. When hung side by side, *Intérieur au teintures roses I* and *II* form one image. The shoulder of the figure in the right panel is seen as a violin-shaped arabesque in the extreme right corner of the left sheet. Yet Vuillard plays dramatic games here with the alternation of scale. The lamp and figure in *II* are large and take up the entire vertical expanse of the composition. But in the right sheet, *I*, the same lamp is drastically reduced in the composition. Similarly, there is a small figure standing in the doorway. The scale of these two compositions is very different, yet by uniting them, Vuillard creates an energized spatial effect.

4. See Roger-Marx, *L'Oeuvre gravé de Vuillard*, no. 37.

5. Once it is established that this is the same room as the one in *The Window*, for example, the indistinguishable features of the background of this painting can be understood. For example, the brown object behind Marie (the figure in blue) is not the back of her chair but a bureau, on top of which a vase can vaguely be distinguished. The narrow strip of light on

the left of the picture can now be understood to highlight a door frame or different wall, more clearly seen in other paintings of this room. Because of its close connection to these pictures from circa 1893, it is likely that Vuillard painted this work at around the same time. This would date the picture earlier than the assigned 1896.

6. Vuillard's addresses, most of which are already known, were found in the *Bottin Commercial* from 1877 until 1898, the last year his mother was registered as a *corsetière*. Vuillard recorded his addresses in some of his diaries (that of 1907 has a list of most of the apartments), but these prove to be not entirely accurate when compared to the concrete information provided by the *Bottins*. More detailed information about the buildings and apartments in which Vuillard lived can be found in the census surveys, the so-called *Calepins cadastres*, located in Archives de la Seine, the archives of the city of Paris. Unfortunately, these cadastral surveys no longer exist for every street in Paris. The surveys in 1862 and 1876 include thorough descriptions of the buildings and an update on the occupants, but that of 1900 lists neither the occupants nor the specific number of rooms and windows.

The 1862 census survey records the following description of 346, rue St. Honoré (Calepins cadastres Serie D1P4, rue St. Honoré, 1862):

Maison avec entrée de porte cochère, ayant 6 croisées de face au 1er étage, faite en pierres de taille, moellons et pans de bois, double en profondeur ayant en aile à d.te un batîment simple en profondeur elevée sur caves d'un rez-de-chaussée, d'un entresol, de 2 étages carrés et d'un 3ème mansarde.
Escalier clair et commode fait en liais jusqu'au 1er et ensuite en bois.
Au fond de la cour, batîment double en profondeur élevé sur caves d'un rez-de-chaussée et 4 étages.
Escalier en bois, clair et commode.

7. The 1876 census survey only reached 200, rue St. Honoré, but the 1862 survey records the following description of 342, rue St. Honoré (Calepins cadastres, Serie D1P4, la rue St. Honoré, 1862):

Cette maison a son entrée par une porte d'allée le n. 344. Elle est faite en pierre de taille, moellons et pans de bois: Elle est double en profondeur, elle a deux croisées en face au premier étage. Elle a une aile à gauche la cage à l'escalier, elle est élevée sur caves d'un rez-de-chaussée, de 4 étages carrés et d'un 5 en retrait et d'un 6ème sous comble.
Elle a au fond de la cour un batîment double en profondeur, élevé sur caves d'un rez-de-chaussée, de 4 étages carrés et d'un 5e mansarde et d'un 6ème sous comble. L'escalier qui dessert ces batîments est fait en bois. Il est claire et commode.
Il y a une boutique et locations pour sentiers industriels et ouvriers.

8. For the families Desmarais, Natanson, Vaquez, and Anet. These are the subject of a thesis now being completed by Gloria Groom. All but one of the commissions had been completed by this time; those for Anet would be finished in the following year.

9. The only exception to this was the three years when the family lived on the rue de Miromesnil, a little farther up the street, off the Faubourg St. Honoré.

10. ". . . un vieux droit de bourgeoisie qui remonte haut dans l'histoire de Paris." Louis Lurine, *Les rues de Paris: Paris ancien et moderne, origines, histoire, monuments, costumes, moeurs, chroniques, et traditions* (Paris, 1884), p. 331.

11. Lurine, p. 332.

Les marchands, principalement les drapiers, les fourreurs, les brodeurs et ce qui vendaient de riches étoffes ou d'autres objets de luxe, suivirent l'exemple des seigneurs qui les enrichissaient; derrière les hôtels et les palais des nobles, surgit cette longue rue St. Honoré, semblable à ces grands fleuves qui traversent tout un empire, en lui apportant la richesse et la fertilité.

12. Lurine, p. 339.

De l'Oratoire de Protestants jusqu'à Saint Roch, la rue St. Honoré est plus bariolé, plus changeant et plus luxueuse. L'aristocratie commerciale s'y fait sentir: ce sont, pour la plupart, des marchands de fourures precieuses, de riches orfêvres, des horlogers et des magasins de nouveautés.

13. Lurine, p. 341.

Nous sommes presque forcés de changer de plume: le vieux Paris cesse; plus de marchands, plus de commerce, plus de ruines, tout est neuf: moeurs, aspect, temples et palais.

14. Lurine, p. 341.

. . . s'élargit et attire les regards par sa splendeur et son opulence.

15. Lurine, p. 338.

Quoique cette immense rue soit encore célèbre par son commerce, elle a beaucoup perdu son caractère primitif . . . on n'y retrouve maintenant que les gros bourgeois, le boutiquier, hélas!

16. I would like to thank Maureen Cassidy-Geiger of the department of European Sculpture and Decorative Arts at The Metropolitan Museum of Art for helping me identify styles, trends, and sources in this chapter.

17. Lucien Magne, "L'Art dans l'habitation moderne," *Revue des arts décoratifs*, vol. 5 (1884–85), p. 98.

Et comme la raison des oeuvres anciennes est bien interpretée! Vous voulez au plafond des solives apparentes; mais vos solives sont en carton-pâté, et comme elles pourraient tomber si elles étaient trop saillantes, vous n'avez que des moitiés de solives. Vous voulez une cheminée monumentale; mais comme elle n'a pas été construite avec le mur, son coffre est trop étroit et la fumée n'est pas évacuée. D'ailleurs, pour éviter d'écraser le plancher, votre cheminée est réduite a une méchante armature de bois ou de fer, enduite de plâtre, mais peinte et dorée. Vos marbres sont en stuc, vos sculptures en patisserie, vos vitraux en papier transparent. Vienne le tappissier qui completera cet ensemble par quelques teintures banales et quelques meubles de pacotille, et voilà ce qu'on est convenu d'appeler l'art dans la maison.

18. Magne, p. 98.

son goût pour le bibelot, pour la fausse archéologie, à son ignorance des règles les plus elementaires de la critique artistique:

L'imitation d'une oeuvre d'art est une chose absurde, parce qu'il est impossible de rencontrer, à deux époques différentes, des besoins et des idées absolument identiques, exigeant la même expression. Mais ce qui est bien pis [*sic*] que l'imitation, c'est association, dans une oeuvre moderne, de morceaux empruntés à des oeuvres à des civilisations différentes. Comment! non contents d'appartenir au XIXe siècle, vous voulez réunir dans vos maisons les portiques de Pompei, la salle à manger de Henri II, le salon de Louis XIV et le boudoir de Louis XV?

19. Magne, p. 98:

Tout besoin peut trouver une expression décorative; tout oeuvre peut affecter une forme qui détermine son caractère artistique.

20. *Woman in Blue (At the Ransons')* (private collection) from about 1900, for example, depicts a gathering of women at Paul Ranson's apartment on the Boulevard Montparnasse, the "temple" where the Nabis had gathered in the earlier years of the decade. Like Vuillard's photographs of his own apartment, this painting reveals an interior filled with pictures hanging on the wall. Some of these paintings have been identified in *Edouard Vuillard, Ker-Xavier Roussel*, p. 100.

21. For further information see P. Verneuil, "Les Etoffes teintes d'Isaac," *Art et Décoration*, vol. 1 (1897), pp. 49–56.

22. Mario Praz, *An Illustrated History of Furnishing from the Renaissance to the Twentieth Century* (New York: George Braziller, 1964), p. 371.

23. Magne, p. 98. He added:

> Vous imposez à l'architecte la réproduction de ces formes, absolument incompatibles avec les besoins de votre habitation.

24. Jean Schopfer (Claude Anet), "Modern Decoration," *The Architectural Record,* vol. 6, no. 3 (January-March 1897), p. 247. It is interesting that the author chose to illustrate several examples of plates that Vuillard had designed for him as an example of "modern decoration."

25. Thiebault-Sisson, "A propos d'une décoration d'interieur: Pourquoi d'art nouveau, chez nous, est en retard . . . ," *Art et Décoration* (1897), pp. 25–29.

26. Under the influence of William Morris some wallpaper had ceased in the 1860s to create tactile, three-dimensional illusions of flowers or other natural forms and began to respect the flatness of the wall. By the end of the century, of course, art nouveau wallpapers were often seen in Parisian apartments, but Vuillard's choice—or his landlord's—was different. The dark colors of these walls, in which brown, burgundy, and beige predominate, reflect the taste for covering dining room walls with embossed leather, which was easy to wipe clean of smoke and grease. Yet the photograph shows these walls were lined in paper, designed to create the same visual effect as embossed leather.

27. Anna Chave refers to its "considerable size and austere plainness" in "Vuillard's *La Lampe," Yale University Art Gallery Bulletin,* Fall 1980, p. 14.

28. Photographs are a continuing source of information about the apartments Vuillard painted, but in addition to the distortions inherent in the medium, they only reveal as much as the photographer chose to depict. For an idea of the complete environment, other documents are necessary.

29. EV I.2, 50v–52 (26 October 1894):

> Sur la table à midi les chrysanthèmes violacées et blanches. Motif ornemental sérieux et aimable à la fois. Décoration de bureau. Les fleurs après tout sont un ornement grossier, simple, je ne veux pas dire que je les méprise, mais cela ne demande aucun effort pour en saisir l'aspect, les formes et les couleurs, c'est proprement le véritable ornement naturel Le sens ornemental en est primitif, simple, a un intérêt suffisant dans la qualité de leurs formes et de leurs couleurs; tout au contraire un tableau qui lui aussi se constitue de formes et de couleurs demande à l'esprit qui le contemple un effort d'imagination plus complexe. D'autres objets une figure, un pot, par exemple l'intérêt ornemental en est moins brutal, ce ne sont pas des couleurs vives, il n'y a pas une répétition multiple de formes semblables (comme les pétales). Quel danger d'attacher plus d'importance aux idées, qu'à la cause qui les fait naître. Et combien il est naturel à ma faiblesse d'y tomber toujours. Ainsi cette idée de la vie qui nous entoure de notre vie, source de toutes nos réflexions et productions, cela devient le modernisme (les tableaux d'intérieur (sens journal) un poncif dont la compréhension devient aussi brumeuse que les autres.
> Ce matin dans mon lit en me réveillant je regardais les objets différents qui m'entouraient, les plafond peint en blanc, l'ornement du milieu arabesques vaguement XVIIIᵉ siècle, l'armoire à glace en face, les rainures, moulures du bois, celles de la fenêtre, leurs proportions, les *rideaux,* la chaise par devant à dossier bois scuplté, le papier du mur, les boutons de la porte ouverte, verre et cuivre, le bois du lit, le bois du paravent, les charnières, mes vêtements au pied du lit; les quatre feuilles vertes élégantes dans un pot, l'encrier, les livres, les rideaux de l'autre fenêtre, les murs de la cour au travers, les différences de perspectives à travers les 2 fenêtres, l'une avec une petite découpure de ciel à lignes parallèles à celles de la fenêtre, dans l'autre, faisant un angle perpendiculaire, l'impression qui résulte de ce coin là seulement. (Quant aux rideaux, différences et dessins obtenus par le plus ou moins d'écartement des fils. Comparant les qualités de chacun de ces objets à cela

seul j'éprouve un plaisir. Puis j'étais frappé par l'abondance d'ornements de tous ces objets. Il sont ce que l'on appelle de mauvais goût et ils ne me seraient pas familiers qu'ils me seraient peut être insupportables. C'est l'occasion de réfléchir sur cette appellation que je dis rapidement "de mauvais goût" et qui m'empêche de regarder. Là je *regardais* et cela ne choquait pas mes nerfs superficiellement je prenais intérêt à chacun de leurs caractères, et cela suffisait à éloigner le dégoût. Ne pas se laisser aller à ces impressions de petit maître comme on aurait dit autrefois; tâcher au contraire à en comprendre le caractère; c'est aussi difficile, même plus je crois, mais très instructif de comprendre une chose vulgaire, (je ne dis plus simple) une chose commune qu'une belle chose consacrée qui vois a ému. Comprendre le monde ainsi, c'était je crois la tentative qu'indiquaient primitivement ceux qui parlaient les premiers de moderne et de modernité. Ils étaient sûrs de trouver dans cette étude sincère et sans préjugés de grandes émotions et des sujets parfois très grands non toujours ridicules. Le ridicule est une chose peut-être aussi tourmentante aussi déprimante pour l'esprit qui le sent et le montre dans les autres que pour ceux qui en sont victimes. A force de sentir les ridicules on arrive à ne plus pouvoir fixer son attention sur rien. Vraiment ce matin le résultat de toutes ces observations n'était pas un dégoût, une acceptation qui plus forte m'eut peut-être donné des idées plus fécondes. Autre chose encore, j'ai été étonné de voir arriver au milieu de ces objets maman dans un peignoir bleu à raies blanches. Somme toute pas un de ces objets inanimés n'avait un rapport ornemental simple avec un autre, l'ensemble était disparate au dernier point. Pourtant cela était dans une atmosphère vive une impression particulière s'en dégageait qui ne m'était pas désagréable. L'arrivée de maman là dedans était surprenante, une personne vivante. En tant que peintre les différences de taches, de forme suffisent pour intéresser.

30. Chave (pp. 12–15) observed that Vuillard has introduced a literal excuse for her bending over in the form of a flower that has fallen to the floor.

31. It has been said that her pose reflects that of Ingres's painting of M. Bertin, which hung in the Louvre and which has always been seen as an iconic image of an authority figure.

32. The bureau is a dominant feature in many paintings of Vuillard's mother and sister and is usually placed to give solidity and a sense of immutability to Mme. Vuillard.

33. The skeletal faces in Vuillard's paintings from this time often resemble those in Munch's paintings from the 1890s. For the connections between Munch and Vuillard, see the chapter "Munch und Vuillard" in Henning Bock and Günther Busch, eds. *Edvard Munch. Problema-Forschungen-Thesen.* Studien zur Kunst des neunzehnen Jarhunderts (Munich), vol. 21 (1973).

34. George Mauner has written about one of these drawings and its relation to some of the paintings discussed here in "Vuillard's Mother and Sister Paintings and the Symbolist Theatre," *Artscanada,* vol. 28, no. 162/163 (December 1971/January 1972), pp. 125ff. For a more extensive discussion of Vuillard's illustrations for the theater, see Genevieve Aitken, "Les peintres et le théâtre autour de 1900 à Paris," Ecole du Louvre, 1978. Although she relates Vuillard's lithographs to the plot of the play for which the illustration was intended, she does not extend her discussion to Vuillard's painted compositions. Anne Georges also outlines the relationship of Vuillard's work to the activities of Symbolist theater in Paris. Belinda Thompson devoted a chapter to Vuillard's work in the theater in *Vuillard,* which appeared as this book went to press. There is still, however, much work to be done on the connection between Vuillard's paintings of the 1890s and the plays with which he was most involved. Themes of isolation, contemplation, and alienation that were central to the plays of Maeterlinck, Beaubourg, and Ibsen were clearly inspirational to Vuillard who sought similar moods for his work. Maurice Maeterlinck in "A propos de Solness Le Constructeur" (*Le Figaro,* April 2, 1894) wrote

eloquently about the poetry of nonaction and the dramatic aspects of the everyday:

> Il m'est arrivé de croire qu'un vieillard assis dans son fauteuil, attendant simplement sous la lampe, écoutant sans le savoir toutes les lois éternelles qui regnent autour de sa maison, interpretant sans le comprendre ce qu'il y a dans le silence des portes et des fenêtres et dans la petite voix de la lumière, subissant la presence de son âme et de sa destinée, . . . il m'est arrivé de croire que ce vieillard immobile vivait en réalité d'une vie plus profonde, plus humaine et plus generale que l'amant qui étrangle sa maitresse.

35. Mauner, pp. 124–26.

36. Oil on canvas, 1890, Paris, Musée d'Orsay, R.F. 2791.

37. See Roger-Marx, *L'Oeuvre gravé de Vuillard,* no. 10.

38. See Russell, no. 29.

The Music of Painting: Homages to Misia

Qui dit un art dit une poésie. Il n'y a pas d'art sans un but poétique. Il y a un genre d'émotion qui est tout particulièr à la peinture. Il y a une impression qui résulte de tel arrangement de couleurs, de lumières, d'ombres etc. C'est ce qu'on appellerait la musique du tableau.
EV I.2, 68 (January 1894)

1. Bret Waller, "La Revue Blanche," in *Artists of La Revue Blanche* (Rochester: Memorial Art Gallery of the University of Rochester, 1984), p. 9.

2. The idea of the arabesque had been explored thoroughly by the Wagnerian music critics by the mid-nineteenth century. In the 1854 *Vom Musikalisch-Schonen,* for example, Edouard Hanslick described the "musical idea," which

> reproduced in its entirety is not only an object of intrinsic beauty but also an end in itself, and not a means for representing thoughts and feelings. The essence of music is sound and motion. The arabesque, a branch of the art of ornamentation, dimly betokens in what manner music may exhibit forms of beauty though no definite emotion be involved.

Joseph Masheck ("The Carpet Paradigm: Critical Prolegomena to a Theory of Flatness," *Artsmagazine,* vol. 51 [September 1976], pp. 82–109) has seen in Hanslick's writing an important source for the *Introduction à une esthétique scientifique* written in 1885 by Charles Henry, an avant-garde scientist and aesthetician. This text, which Seurat had read as well, exerted a seminal influence on the Nabis; Vuillard was certainly familiar with it.
Masheck has discussed the roots of musicality in the arabesque. He links Delacroix's use of the term "arabesque" to the critic Jean-Louis Pleisse's concept of musicality, referred to in a review of Delacroix's work from the Salon of 1849. Masheck also mentions Maurice Denis's appreciation for "les arabesques bleues" of the Mona Lisa.

3. EV I.2, 68 (January 1894):

> L'impression qu'on reçoit par les beaux arts n'a pas le moindre rapport avec le plaisir que fait éprouver une imitation quelconque Qui dit un art dit une poésie. Il n'y a pas d'art sans un but poétique. Il y a un genre d'émotion qui est tout particulièr à la peinture. Il y a une impression qui résulte de tel arrangement de couleurs, de lumières, d'ombres etc. C'est qu'on appellerait la musique du tableau.

"Delacroix" is written sideways along passage.

4. Charles Baudelaire, "Correspondances" in *Oeuvres Complètes* (Paris: Gallimard, 1975–76), vol. I, p. 11.

5. G. Albert Aurier, "Le Symbolisme en peinture: Paul Gauguin," *Mercure de France,* March 1891; cited in Robert Goldwater, *Symbolism,* New York: Harper & Row, 1979, pp. 183–84.

6. EV I.2, 44 (16 July 1894):

> Visite hier à Cluny. Les tapisseries et les eluminures de missel. Calendriers. Dans les tapisseries je pense qu'en grandissant purement et simplement mon petit panneau cela ferait le sujet d'une décoration. Sujets humbles de ces décorations de Cluny! Expression d'un *sentiment intime* sur une plus grande surface voilà tout. La même chose qu'un Chardin par exemple . . . Petit morceau trés ancien, en teintes plates grossières, d'un charme de couleur très puissant couleurs tranchées sur fond clair . . . Il y a deux occupations en moi: l'étude de la perception extérieure remplie d'expériences pénibles et dangereuses pour mon humeur et mes nerfs. l'étude de la décoration picturale rarement possible du reste bien plus bornée mais qui devrait me donner la tranquillité d'un ouvrier—repenser souvent aux tapisseries de Cluny . . .

It is interesting to note that in thinking of these tapestries Vuillard reflects on the approach to subject matter of large decoration and the work of Sérusier and Denis:

> Autrefois Sérusier moi n'y prêtant pas trop d'attention croyant l'avoir déjà compris parlant de l'intérêt de la nature morte et de l'indifférence à ces sujets pompeux italiens. Pensant à décorer un salon avec des marchandes de pots. Peu importe l'objet. C'est son sujet qui est tout. Et Denis faisant cette réflexion: comme il suffit d'agrandir un petit dessin. à propos de Michel Ange. Et dernièrement l'exemple de Forain au café riche. Et moi-même dans mon paravent de Me. Desmarais. J'ai fait cela sans y penser !!!! J'en prends conscience maintenant seulement.

7. There is a possibility that this is not a tapestry but a large decorative painting. The scene, though difficult to decipher, shows figures dancing in a ring, with a lake in the distance surrounded by trees. This does not resemble any known works by Vuillard, but could possibly be a large composition by Ker-Xavier Roussel, who specialized in scenes of nymphs and satyrs in idyllic surroundings.

8. Stuart Preston hypothesized that Misia was listening to an unseen musician playing the piano. While there is no absolute evidence against this proposal, it should be noted that Vuillard never showed anyone but Misia at her piano.

9. EV I.2, 57v (24 December 1896):

> Thadée et sa femme très bon moment. Attendrissement désirs de travail, ambitions et sensualités. rentré à 4 heures, dormi jusqu'à midi. Incertitudes et désirs contraires. Abondance de souvenirs.

10. EV, Institut de France, inv. no. 5397, carnet 2, 1908:

> Après à l'atelier travaillé avec un photo et un pastel d'été.

11. The only publication on Vuillard's photographs is the catalogue from a small exhibition from 1963: "Vuillard et son Kodak," *L'Oeil* (Paris: Galerie d'Art, 1963). Annette Vaillant, daughter of Alfred Natanson, provided some commentary, along with short anecdotes by Jacques Salomon. This catalogue focused on the appearance of the same people in both paintings and photographs. The captions identified who was in the picture or where it was taken.
Some photographs are juxtaposed with paintings whose composition appears to be the same. Yet a photograph of Mme. Vuillard drinking coffee is placed next to a painting from almost a decade before. No direct causal connection can thus be made between the paintings and photographs. This catalogue is still a valuable resource because so few of Vuillard's photographs are available for study. I am grateful to Antoine Salomon for making his private archive of Vuillard's photographs available to me.

12. See Eugenia Parry Janis, "Edgar Degas' Photographic Theater," in Jacqueline and Maurice Guillaud, eds., *Degas: Form and Space* (Paris and New York: Guillaud Editions and Rizzoli, 1984), pp. 451–86. Janis outlines with great care Degas's photography and its relation to contemporary experimentation in the medium.

13. Janis, p. 466.

14. Like Vuillard, Degas was closely tied to Mallarmé in the 1890s. Degas took a photograph of the poet, posed with the painter Renoir, while Vuillard painted pictures of his house and planned to illustrate his *Hérodiade*.

15. J. T. Kirk Varnadoe, "The Artifice of Candor: Impressionism and Photography Reconsidered," *Art in America*, vol. 68 (January 1980), p. 69.

16. The connection to Vuillard is twofold: a similar disturbance takes place in Vuillard's paintings where the foreground figure is large and the background figure is small; it is as if the foreground figure has blocked out the depth of field. In addition, the large size of the foreground figure implies Vuillard's extreme proximity to it, and this could also account for the minimizing of the background figures.

17. Dom W. Verkade, *Le tourment de Dieu, étapes d'un moine peintre* (Paris, 1923), p. 94.

18. Vuillard might have been inspired by the scratching inherent in printmaking to use it for great effect in his oils.

19. The preference for the Gothic of A. W. N. Pugin and Owen Jones ruled wallpaper design from the 1850s into the 1870s and thus did away with the Naturalist tendencies in French wallpaper that had dominated the earlier part of the century. Pugin and Jones called for a strict formalism in domestic decoration where the flatness of the wall had to be respected and where flowers and birds should only be represented in a conventional way. William Morris tended to take an opposite route and, in the 1880s and 1890s, combined naturalistic three-dimensional representations of flowers with more abstract patterns of vines behind them. This combination of Naturalism and artifice, along with a taste for an asymmetrical mise-en-scene, was due to the joint influence of Japanese design and Renaissance ornament.

See Peter Floud, "The Wallpaper Designs of William Morris," *The Penrose Annual*, vol. 54 (1960), pp. 41–45. Catherine W. Lynn's *Wallpaper in America* (New York: W. W. Norton, 1980) was also very helpful in setting the context of French late nineteenth century styles.

20. These figures were identified in *Edouard Vuillard, Ker-Xavier Roussel*, p. 77.

21. Roger-Marx, *L'Oeuvre gravé de Vuillard*, p. 48, no. 12. Aside from the two easily seen on either side of the lamp, the back of a woman's head can be seen at the lower left, with two figures depicted without color and with just a few marks of the crayon under the lampshade.

Conclusion

1. See *The Selected Writings of Hermann von Helmholtz* (Middletown, Conn.: Weslayen University Press, 1971).

2. Robert L. Herbert, lectures, Yale University, 1980.

APPENDIX A

VUILLARD'S CHRONOLOGIES

Vuillard made two chronologies of important events in his life. They are both included in this book because of their critical importance to future scholarship on Vuillard. The first, probably from 1905, is found in EV I.2, 77v–78.

77v

	90	année de Serusier
	89	portrait Waroq. dessin salon. flemme de Mouclier
		école
		petites salissures de mémoire
		2 mois de service
mi-avril 88		passage à l'Ecôle cours du soir vitraux natures mortes. leçons
rue du Marché 87		Julian natures mortes de la salle à manger
		Baudry reçu à l'Ecôle en juillet
		entrée a l'Ecôle vitraux
nov. 85–86		Louvre voyage à Cuiseaux 2 échecs
		à l'Ecôle entrée chez Julian

78

21	90	Serusier. rue Miromesnil mansarde, atelier de Ranson
22	91	hiv? rue Miromesnil (?) atelier rue Pigalle Lugné Bonnard G. Roussel oct. au 24
23	92	hiver triste dessins et pochades Dessus de porte Desmarais Kerr et Caro Voyage
24	93	paravent mariage de Mimi. série de petites peintures, l'oeuvre
25	94	histoires sentimentales. panneaux d'Al.-Natanson
*95		panneaux de Thadée histoires de Marie _____ ?
96		panneaux de Vaquez Valvins, Cuiseaux

97	exposition Vollard lithographies Villeneuve
98	panneau Schopfer Villeneuve 28 jours naissance d'Annette
99	exposition Durand Ruel Londres Bibesco Bernheim. panneaux de la rue Jouffroy
1900	exposition avril chez Bernheim panneau Aghion, Etang la Ville Suisse / Romanel
1901	midi Espagne jaunisse indépandants Feydeau. Vasouy panneau Schopfer
1902	Indépendants Bernheim Etincelles
1903	Indépendants Bernheim Vasouy
1904	Salon Automne Vasouy

The second chronology dates from 11–12 November 1908 and is found in EV inv. no 5397, carnet 2, page 12. It corroborates in most respects the list from the earlier journal. But at times Vuillard's memory is mistaken. For example, he lists under 1891 the rue de Miromesnil in the earlier journal and the rue St. Honoré in the later journal. The Bottin confirms that in 1891 the Vuillard family would be found in the rue de Miromesnil.

85 november quitte Condorcet. rue du Marché St. Honoré traîne au Louvre deux échecs à l'Ecôle en 86. voyage à Cuiseaux grace à la tante Saurel. entrée chez Julian

87 rue du Marché St. Honoré. Julian espacé. natures mortes de la salle à manger. Baudry. vitraux
collections du père Roussel. reçu a l'Ecôle en juillet apres 3 échecs.
octobre rue Miromesnil.

143

88 passage à l'Ecôle. Gérôme 6 semaines. cours Yven et Monparnasse. vitraux. natures mortes. leçons de dessin

89 rue Miromesnil. portrait de Waroquy dans la chambre de bonne maman. Mouclier. Année de l'exposition reçu dessin de bonne maman au salon.
promenades commence à travailler de mémoire. petites salissures. à la fin nov. et décembre service militaire à Lisieux

90 connaissance de Sérusier. Bonnard par Denis. rue de Miromesnil. mansarde. atelier de Ranson l'été Lugné-Poe. Darzens. campagne à St. Maurice. Créteil.

91 rue St. Honoré 346. atelier 28 Pigalle Natanson avec Lugné. Bonnard et Georges Roussel. en octobre seul à 24.

92 hiver triste dessins et pochades. Dessus de porte de Madame Desmarais. Kerr et Caro. voyage en Belgique Hollande et Londres

93 paravent de Madame Desmarais. Vallotton. Mariages de Thadée. De Denis et de Kerr. série de petites peintures l'oeuvre. mort de bonne maman en janvier.

94 histoires sentimentales. september août panneaux d'Alexandre Natanson

95 complications du ménage Roussel. panneaux de Thadée novembre (atelier. boulevard de Clichy?). Vaquez. mort de ma tante Saurel. avril à Berde chez Malaquin

96 rue St. Honoré 342. panneaux de Vaquez atelier chambre rue Drouot mois d'août. Valvins juillet. voyage à Cuiseaux. Valvins oct à déc. mort du petit jean

97 exposition Vollard. lithographies Villeneuve sur Yonne

98 Voyage Italie Venise et Florence. Denis et Schopfer. panneaux Schopfer 28 jours Villeneuve naissance d'Annette novembre rue des Batignolles

99 exposition Durand-Ruel. voyage à Londres avec Bonnard. Bibesco, les Bernheim. panneaux de la rue Jouffroy. les Roussel à Levallois et juin à l'Etang la Ville. en Mars 99 rue Truffaut. automne merveilleux à Villeneuve voyage en avril à Milan et à Venise avec Bonnard et K.

1900 exposition en avril chez les Bernheim panneau d'Aghion atelier rue Nollet 6 mois. Etang la Ville. la Suisse et Romanel. Misia près de Bade. à Cannes hotel

1901 Cannes la croix des gardes. voyage avec Bibesco et Bonnard en Espagne. jaunisse. exposition independants. Feydeau. la Terrasse à Vasouy. panneau Schopfer.
avril 1901 installation des Roussel à l'Etang

1902 les Independants. les Bernheim. les Etincelles. Villerville avec les Roussel

1903 Indépendants. Bernheim. Vasouy. Voyage à Vienne Misia et Thadée. hiver 03 à 4 Ker à St. Tropez.

1904 Salon d'automne achat du Luxembourg. Vasouy octobre rue de la Tour. St. Tropez au printemps.

1905 Amfréville. modèles rue de la Tour. peintures ches les Fontaine (ventes aux Bernheim. prince de Wagram Dutil. mariages Natanson Fénéon)

1906 Amfréville. Bretagne. Fontaine. Favet Claude Bernheim. travail en ville. Voyage à Ventnor en avril voyage à Bagnoles auto en juin. 13 jours à Alencon. voyages en auto

1907 Amfréville. portrait de Marthe Bonnard. du petit Gangnat-Cadet. voyages en auto le dimanche. à Dieppe avec les Philippi portrait d'Olga Natanson. pastels. paysages. retour à la colle d'été.

1908 rue de Calais juillet. Pouliguen. phlébites de Kerr legère en juillet. grave en oct. nov. décembre. expositions panneaux Bibesco. au début de l'année exposition retrospective et du Pouliguen en nov. chez Bernheim. Nouvel arrangement d'affaires avec les Bernheim à partir de juillet. octobre nov. déc. phlébite double de Kerr voyage à l'Etang. lectures.

(95) service de table de Schopfer. 28 jours à Nancy Stéph ler déjeuner chez Hessel rue d'Argenteuil. départ fugue de Kerr 16 juillet retour place Dauphine en octobre.
acheteurs. Hayen 4 Sako 23. Vollard (estampes 5-Level 1 Mellerio 15. Vaquez 10 total 2400

(98) acheteur Vollard 1320. Bernheim 300 Schopfer 900 Gallimard 450 total 2740

APPENDIX B

VUILLARD'S VISITS TO THE LOUVRE

In his journals from 1888 to 1905, Vuillard writes of repeated, daily trips to the Louvre in 1888 and 1894. The following is a list of these references. Given that he visited the museum almost daily in later life, one assumes he also made frequent trips during the 1890s which remain unrecorded.

EV I.1, November 1888

9   dessins d'albert Dürer Holbein [with sketches]

10   Rien que du blue et ou jaune acquarelle ombres transparentes du Louvre [with outside sketches]

10v   Les Ostade du Louvre, les Memling [with sketches] petites Corot lumière du jour Louvre dans l'ombre silence . . . éclairage doré . . . petit rembrandt beauté de la vierge.

11v   après midi au Louvre les Steen éclairages à la Besnard et Chardin . . . ingres . . . Van dyck.

13v   visite au Louvre, les Gerard Dou, le pauvre pecheur.

14v   bibliothèque traité de Leonard Vinci, Poussin, Holbein, Passion musicale.

16   dessin avec Holbein et Cranach . . . en tête pas vu d'ensemble pas de forme comparée . . . les théories prennent le dessus; au Louvre la joconde élégance.

16v   Vierge au voile l'enfant le cou de la vierge Sa bouche, lumière sur la jambe du gosse Rembrandt . . . fin la jaconde. mais tout vu par le détail . . .

December 1888

19v   au Louvre . . . Le Lesueur coloration superbe . . . la messe tout rempli avec des couleurs à la Véronèse la mort de Saphire de Poussin point perspectif . . . furie des Sabins

21v-22r   Après-midi au Louvre cadres brillants calme Ombres lumière du tableau hollandais (famille du charpentier

23v   au Louvre compris la Joconde plus completement en commençant par le coin de bouche familier

25v   au Louvre idee de force dans la tête jeune tableau carré allure tranquille de Leon d'Este bouche palpitante type quelquepeu décoratif moment de contemplation instruction—après la Joconde le portrait de Rembrand plus calme plus sérieux encore . . .

31   Sentiment fier de la belle Jardiniere.

32   visite au Louvre   les Lesueur   coloration établissement les Millet.

EV I.2, 13 July 1894

42v–43

L'après-midi promenade au Louvre avec Bonnard dans les dessins d'abord. Ennui rapide devant les italiens. Quel mensonge que d'appeler cela des primitifs. Quoi de plus rhétorique, de moins ému que Credi, Botticelli (je parle du dessin de la première salle) Pisano, les dessins de Signorelli.) à part le Taddeo Gaddi. Réflexion de Bonnard. Toute l'impression que donne ce dessin a-t-elle été consciente quelle est la part du temps, en dehors de la forme la couleur peut elle lui être attribuée. Bonnard: jamais de doute de ce genre devant un japonais.
Intérêt reprend un peu devant Léonard. au moins cette rhétorique sert-elle là a une émotion, se rapprochant du reste des véritables primitifs.
Satisfaction dans la nouvelle salle française, quelle différence d'expression l'arabesque italienne murale devient une image de livre. l'emphase est remplacée par le recueillement la simplicité aimable. Comme les caractères

se perpétuent dans un race, même devant ces dessins quelconques de Coypel cela m'a frappé. Watteau cela semble une singerie ironique de ces sentiments méridionaux par un français ironique la femme de dos en noir. Côté flamand. Réveillé un peu par ces idées du mauvais début de notre visite (la sculpture française !!!!! qui suait l'ennui), quelle vilaines salles, rencontre d'un camarade d'atelier, le comble, la pluie) retour par la salle Lacaze Quel plaisir devant de la peinture, décidément cela me plaît à coeur. La réunion dans un parc! l'indifférent, les petits Ostade Difficulté encore de voir le sujet de Watteau d'une façon pratique. Demi lucidité, demi duperie.

EV I.2, 19 May 1895
56v

Ce matin passe au Louvre. Zurburan, Rubens les trouve laids désagréables et pourtant puissants couleur, formes, ensembles significatifs entiers, évocateur. et significatifs dans leurs bavardages, femmes, chairs, vraiment l'apothéose du musclé, du relief l'amour du relief en dirige la production d'abord. Arrêté par les croisés Delacroix couleurs séduisantes formes aussi libres fantaisistes mais plus touchantes pour moi peut-être par des motifs simplement.

SELECTED BIBLIOGRAPHY

Works about Vuillard

Aitken, Genviève. "Les Peintres et le théâtre à Paris autour de 1900." Diplôme de l'Ecole du Louvre, 1978.

Bacou, Roseline. "Décors d'appartements au temps des Nabis." *Art de France*, 4 (1964): 190–205.

Barilli, Renato. "Bonnard, Vuillard e la poetica degli interni." *Arte Moderna* 2, no. 13 (1967).

Bauman, Felix Andreas. "Edouard Vuillard, Grand intérieur aux six personnages, 1897." *Jahresbericht der Züricher Kunstgesellshaft*, 1966.

Bonnard, Vuillard et les Nabis (1888–1903). Exh. cat. Paris: Musée National d'Art Moderne, 1955.

Chassé, Charles. *The Nabis and Their Period*. Translated by Michael Bullock. New York: Praeger, 1969.

Chastel, André. *Vuillard 1868–1940*. Paris: Floury, 1946.

———. "Vuillard et Mallarmé." *La Nef*, no. 26 (January 1947), pp. 13–25.

———. "Vuillard." *Art News Annual*, 23 (1954): 26–57.

Chave, Anna. "Vuillard's *La Lampe*." *Yale University Art Gallery Bulletin*, 38 (Fall 1980).

Coolus, Romain. "Edouard Vuillard." *Mercure de France*, 1934, pp. 67–68.

Dugdale, James. *Vuillard* (The Masters series, no. 97). London, 1967.

———. "Vuillard, the Decorator." *Apollo* 36 (February 1965): 94–101; *Apollo* 68 (October 1967): 272–77.

Duthuit, G. "Vuillard and the Poets of Decadence." *Art News* 53 (March 1954).

Edouard Vuillard, Ker-Xavier Roussel. Exh. cat. Paris: Orangerie des Tuileries, 1968. Cat. entries by Pierre Georgel.

Georges, Anne. "Symbolisme et décor: Vuillard 1888–1905." Thesis, 3ᵉ cycle, Paris I, 1978.

Mauner, George. *The Nabis: Their History and Their Art 1888–1896*. New York, 1978.

———. "Vuillard's Mother and Sister Paintings and the Symbolist Theatre." *Artscanada*, 28, no. 162–63 (December 1971/January 1972): 124–26.

Natanson, Thadée. *Peints à leur tour*. Paris, 1948.

Oakley, Lucy. *Edouard Vuillard*. New York: The Metropolitan Museum of Art, 1981.

Perucchi-Petri, Ursula. *Die Nabis und Japan: Das Frühwerk von Bonnard, Vuillard und Denis*. Munich: Prestel Verlag, 1976.

Preston, Stuart. *Vuillard*. New York: Abrams, 1971, rev. and abr. London, 1985.

Ritchie, Andrew Carnduff. *Edouard Vuillard*. Exh. cat. Reprint. New York: The Museum of Modern Art, 1954, rpt. 1969.

Roger-Marx, Claude. *L'Oeuvre gravé de Vuillard*. Paris and Monte Carlo: Sauret, 1948.

———. *Vuillard et son temps*. Paris, 1946.

———. *Vuillard: His Life and Work*. London, 1946.

Russell, John. *Vuillard*. London: Thames and Hudson, 1971.

Salomon, Jacques. *Auprès de Vuillard*. Paris, 1953.

———. *Vuillard*. Paris, 1945.

———. *Vuillard*. Paris, 1968.

———. *Vuillard admiré*. Lausanne, 1961.

———. *Vuillard, Douze pastels*. Paris, 1966.

———. *Vuillard: témoignage*. Paris: Michel, 1945.

Salomon, Jacques, and Annette Vaillant. "Vuillard et son Kodak." *L'Oeil*, 100 (April 1963): 14–25, 61.

Schweicher, Curt. *Vuillard*. Bern, 1955.

———. "Die Bildraum Gestaltung das Dekorative und das Ornamentale im Werke von Edouard Vuillard." Thesis, University of Trier, 1949.

Segard, A. *Peintres d'aujourd'hui: Les Décorateurs.* Paris, 1945.

Thompson, Belinda. *Vuillard.* New York: Abbeville Press, 1988.

Vuillard. Exh. cat. Frankfurt: Frankfurter Kunstverein, 1964.

Vuillard: Intérieurs. Lausanne: International Art Book, 1968.

General Works and Related Issues

Alberty. *Guide dans Paris et l'Exposition 1889.* Paris, 1889.

Arguelles, José A. *Charles Henry and the Formation of a Psychophysical Aesthetic.* Chicago: University of Chicago Press, 1972.

Aurier, Albert. *Oeuvres posthumes.* Paris, 1892.

Bachelard, Gaston. *La Poétique de l'éspace.* Paris, 1978.

Barilli, Renato. *Soggettività e oggettività del linguaggio simbolista.* Milan: Fabbri, 1968.

Blanc, Charles. *Grammaire des arts décoratifs, décoration intérieure de la maison.* Paris, 1882.

———. *Grammaire des arts du dessin.* Paris, 1867.

Brücke, Ernst Wilhelm, Ritter von. *Principes scientifique des beaux-arts; essais et fragments de théorie...suivi de l'optique et la peinture, par H. Helmholtz.* 3d ed. Paris: G. Ballière, 1885.

Burhan, Filiz Eda. "Vision and Visionaries: Nineteenth Century Psychological Theory, the Occult Sciences and the Formation of the Symbolist Aesthetic in France." Ph.D. dissertation, Princeton University, 1979.

Chevreul, M.E. *The Laws of Contrast of Color and Their Application to the Arts.* London, 1868.

Clouzot, Henry. *Le Papier peint en France du XVII au XIX siècles.* Paris, 1934.

Copeland, Aaron. *Music and Imagination.* New York, 1959.

Crimp, Douglas. "Positive/Negative. A Note on Degas' Photographs." *October* 5 (Summer 1978): 89–100.

Cunnington, C. Wollett and Phillis. *The History of Underclothes.* London, 1951.

Denis, Maurice. *Théories, 1890–1910: Du Symbolisme et de Gauguin vers un nouvel ordre classique.* Paris: Bibliothèque de l'Occident, 1912.

———. "Définition du néotraditionnisme." *Art et Critique* (August 1890).

Deschaumes, Edmond. *Pour bien voir Paris, guide parisien pittoresque et pratique.* Paris, 1889.

Le Développement de la fabrique et le travail à domicile dans les industries de habillement. Paris, 1906.

Duranty, Louis Emile Edmond. *La Nouvelle peinture, à propos du groupe d'artistes qui expose dans les galeries Durand-Ruel (1876).* New edition, annotated with introduction by Marcel Guérin. Paris: Librarie Floury, 1946.

Ecole Nationale des beaux-arts. *Exposition universelle de 1889. Rapports présentés au conceil d'administration... par les professeurs délégués à l'Exposition.* Paris, 1890.

Fénéon, Félix. *Oeuvres.* Paris, 1948.

Festy, Octave. Ministère du Travail et de la prévoyance sociale. Office du travail. *Enquête sur le travail à domicile dans l'industrie de la lingerie.* Paris, 1907–1911.

Floud, Peter. "The Wallpaper Designs of William Morris." *The Penrose Annual,* 543 (1960).

Focillon, Henri. "L'estampe japonaise et la peinture en Occident dans le 2ᵉ moitié du XIXe siècle." In *Actes du congrès international d'Histoire de l'Art.* Paris, 1921.

Fontainas, A. *Mes souvenirs du symbolisme.* Paris, 1928.

Geffroy, G. *La Vie Artistique.* 8 vols. Paris, 1892–1903.

Ghil, R. *Les Dates et les oeuvres-symbolisme et poème scientifique.* Paris, 1923.

Gide, André. "Promenade au Salon d'Automne." *Gazette des Beaux-Arts,* no. 582 (December 1905).

Goldwater, Robert. *Symbolism.* New York: Harper & Row, 1979.

———. "Symbolist Art and Theater." *Magazine of Art,* 39 (December 1946): 366–70.

Guerinet, Armand. *Intérieurs d'Appartements.* Paris, n.d. [before 1918].

Hare, Augustus J. C. *Walks in Paris.* London, 1888.

Harvard, Henry. *L'Art dans la Maison.* Paris, 1884.

Helmholtz, Hermann Ludwig Ferdinand von. *The Selected Writings of Hermann von Helmholtz.* Middletown, Conn.: Wesleyan University Press, 1971.

Henry, Charles. *Eléments d'une théorie générale de la dynamgenie, autrement dit du contraste, du rythme et de la mesure, avec applications spéciales aux sensations visuelle et auditive.* Paris, 1889.

———. *Harmonies de formes et de couleurs, démonstrations pratiques avec le rapporteur esthétique et le cercle chromatique.* Paris, 1891.

———. *Introduction à une ésthetique scientifique.* Paris, 1885.

———. *Rapporteur esthétique. Notice sur les applications à l'art industriel à l'histoire de l'art, a l'interprétation de la méthode graphique, en général à l'étude et à la rectification esthétique de toutes formes.* Paris, 1888.

Herbert, Eugenia W. *The Artist and Social Reform: France and Belgium, 1885–1898.* New Haven: Yale University Press, 1965.

Herbert, Robert L. *Neo-Impressionism.* Exh. cat. New York: The Solomon R. Guggenheim Museum, 1968.

———. *Neo-Impressionists and Nabis in the Collection of Arthur G. Altschul.* Exh. cat. New Haven: Yale University Art Gallery, 1965.

Hermann, Fritz. *Die Revue Blanche und Die Nabis.* Munich, 1959.

Humbert, Agnes. *Les Nabis et leur époque, 1888–1900.* Geneva: P. Cailler, 1954.

Ives, Colta. *The Great Wave: The Influence of Japanese Woodcuts on French Prints.* Exh. cat. New York: The Metropolitan Museum of Art, 1974.

Janis, Eugenia Parry. "Edgar Degas' Photographic Theater." *Degas: Form and Space,* Jacqueline and Maurice Guillaud, eds. Paris and New York: Guillaud Editions and Rizzoli, 1984.

Kahn, Gustave. *Symbolistes et Décadents.* Paris, 1902.

———. "Réponse des Symbolistes." *L'Evénement* (September 28, 1886).

Lebrun, Mme. P. "Corsetière de Raincy, Banlieu de Paris: veuve travaillant à domicile avec ses enfants, ouvrière à la tâche, proprietaire." In *Les Ouvriers des deux mondes.* Paris: Société d'économie sociale, 1905.

Lockspeiser, Edward. *Music and Painting: A Study in Comparative Ideas from Turner to Schoenberg.* New York: Harper and Row, 1973.

Lurine, Louis. *Les rues de Paris: Paris ancien et moderne, origines, histoire, monuments, costumes, moeurs, chroniques, et traditions.* Paris, 1944.

Lynn, Catherine. *Wallpaper in America.* New York: W.W. Norton, 1980.

Magne, Lucien. "L'Art dans l'habitation Moderne." *Revue des arts décoratifs* 5 (1884–85).

Marx, Roger. "L'Art décoratif et les 'Symbolistes.'" *Le Voltaire,* August 23, 1892.

Masheck, Joseph. "The Carpet Paradigm: Critical Prolegomena to a Theory of Flatness." *Artsmagazine* 51 (September 1976): 82–109.

Matthews, Patricia Townley. *Aurier's Symbolist Art Criticism and Theory.* Ann Arbor, Mich.: UMI Research Press, 1986.

Maus, Octave. *Trente années de lutte pour l'art, 1884–1914.* Brussels, 1926.

Moréas, Jean. "Le Symbolisme." *Figaro Littéraire,* September 18, 1886.

Morin, Louis. *Les Cousettes, Physiologie des couturières de Paris.* Paris, 1895.

Nochlin, Linda. *Impressionism and Post-Impressionism 1874–1904.* Sources and Documents in the History of Art. Englewood Cliffs, N.J.: Prentice-Hall, 1966.

Paris à travers les âges, aspects successifs des monuments et quartiers historiques de Paris depuis le XIIIe siècle jusqu'à nos jours. 2 vols. Paris, 1875–1882.

Post Impressionism. Exh. cat. London: Royal Academy of Art, 1980.

Praz, Mario. *An Illustrated History of Furnishing from the Renaissance to the Twentieth Century.* New York, 1964.

Price, Aimée Brown. *The Decorative Aesthetic in the Work of Pierre Puvis de Chavannes.* Exh. cat. Ottawa: National Gallery of Canada, 1977.

Rewald, John. *Post-Impressionism: From Van Gogh to Gauguin.* New York:

The Museum of Modern Art, 1962.

——. "Excerpts from the unpublished diary of Paul Signac." *Gazette des Beaux-arts*, I (1894–1895), vol. 36 (July-September 1949), pp. 97–128; II (1897–1898), vol. 39 (April 1952), pp. 265–84; III (1898–1899), vol. 42 (July-August 1953).

Richard, V.P. *L'Univers imaginaire de Mallarmé*. Paris.

Rookmaaker, H. R. *Synthetist Art Theories: Genesis and Nature of the Ideas on Art of Gauguin and His Circle*. Amsterdam, 1959.

Sauvage, George. *A Concise History of Interior Decoration*. New York, 1966.

Schopfer, Jean [Claude Anet]. "Modern Decoration." *Architectural Record* 6 (January-March 1897): 240–55.

Seilhac, Léon de. *L'Industrie de la couture et de la confection à Paris*. Paris, 1897.

Sérusier, Paul. *ABC de la peinture*. Paris, 1950.

Signac, Paul. *D'Eugène Delacroix au néo-impressionisme* (1899). Edited by Françoise Cachin. Paris, 1964.

Stein, Jack M. *Richard Wagner and the Synthesis of the Arts*. Detroit: Wayne State University Press, 1960.

Terasse, Antoine. *Degas et la photographie*. Paris, 1983.

Thirion, Yvonne. *De l'influence de l'éstampe japonaise sur la peinture française dans la seconde moitié du XIXe siècle*.

Uzanne, Octave. *La Femme et la mode*. Paris, 1892.

Varnedoe, J. T. Kirk. "The Artifice of Candor: Impressionism and Photography Reconsidered." *Art in America* 68 (January 1980): 66–78.

——. "The Ideology of Time: Degas and Photography." *Art in America* 68 (Summer 1980): 96–110.

Warran, Francis. *L'Oeuvre psychophysique de Charles Henry*. Paris, 1938.

Waugh, Nora. *Corsets and Crinolines*. London, 1954.

INDEX

Page numbers in italics indicate illustrations

150

151

Photography Credits

In most cases, photographs have been supplied by the lenders. We would also like to acknowledge the following photographers: Barney Burstein, Prudence Cuming Associates Limited, Walter Dräyer, Lynton Gardiner, Gerhard Howland, Douglas M. Parker, Studio Lourmel, Eileen Tweedy, and John White.

For permission to reproduce illustrations appearing in this book, please correspond directly with the owners of the works, as listed in the individual captions. The Smithsonian Institution Press does not retain reproduction rights for these illustrations or maintain a file of addresses for photo sources.

This book was designed by Lisa Buck Vann and edited by Carolyn Vaughan and Leigh Alvarado Benson. Polly Koch was assistant editor. Type was set in Garamond #3 by Monotype Composition Company, Inc., Baltimore, Maryland, and the book was printed and bound in Japan by Toppan Printing Company, Ltd.